Midwest Mediterranean

Finding Health & Flavor with the Foods of the North

THERAN PRESS

THERAN PRESS IS THE ACADEMIC PUBLISHING IMPRINT OF SILVER GOAT MEDIA.

THERAN IS DEDICATED TO AUTHENTIC PARTNERSHIPS WITH OUR ACADEMIC ASSOCIATES, TO THE QUALITY DESIGN OF SCHOLARLY BOOKS, AND TO ELITE STANDARDS OF PEER REVIEW.

THERAN SEEKS TO FREE INTELLECTUALS FROM THE CONFINES OF TRADITIONAL PUBLISHING.

THERAN SCHOLARS ARE AUTHORITIES AND REVOLUTIONARIES IN THEIR RESPECTIVE FIELDS.

THERAN ENCOURAGES NEW MODELS FOR GENERATING AND DISTRIBUTING KNOWLEDGE.

FOR OUR CREATIVES, FOR OUR COMMUNITIES, FOR OUR WORLD.

WWW.THERANPRESS.ORG

This book was designed and produced by Silver Goat Media, LLC. Fargo, ND U.S.A. www.silvergoatmedia.com

SGM, the SGM goat, Theran Press, and the Theran theta are trademarks of Silver Goat Media, LLC.

Cover design by Cady Ann Rutter © 2021 SGM
Typeset by Jonathan Rutter © 2021 SGM
Mediterranean diet pyramid by George Middleton © 2009 Oldways Preservation and Exchange Trust

ISBN-13: 978-1-944296-17-9

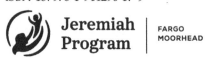

A portion of the annual proceeds from the sale of this book is donated to the Jeremiah Program, Fargo-Moorhead. **www.jeremiahprogram.org**

MIDWEST MEDITERRANEAN

FINDING HEALTH & FLAVOR WITH THE FOODS OF THE NORTH

David Clardy, Megan Myrdal, Fadel Nammour,
Peter Schultz, William Schultz & Noreen Thomas

THERAN PRESS

For our friends, families, farmers, and fellow food lovers
—from the Midwest to the Mediterranean—
and everywhere in between.

❧ TABLE OF CONTENTS

 CONTRIBUTORS

David Clardy (BA, University of Chicago; MD, Washington University, St. Louis) is an adventurer, educator, and physician. He completed his work in Internal Medicine and Cardiology at the University of Chicago's Michael Reese Hospital and Medical Center. He is currently a Clinical Associate Professor at the University of North Dakota and the Medical Director of Cardiovascular Diagnostics and Nuclear Cardiology at Sanford Heart and Vascular Center in Fargo, ND. In addition to patient care, his main research interests are in the fields of cardiac imaging and preventive cardiology.

Megan Myrdal (MS, NDSU; RD, Concordia College) is a registered dietitian, a farmer's daughter, and a general enthusiast for all things food and farming. She's the Co-Founder and Operations Director of Food of the North, a non-profit dedicated to celebrating, connecting, and empowering the food communities of the High Plains. Her work experience has spanned the food industry, including nutrition and culinary education, food system policy, farmers market development, agriculture marketing, and higher education. Throughout her career, Megan has learned that the people who care deeply about food are some of the best folks on the planet; supporting, elevating, and working with this community is the source of her daily motivation.

Fadel Nammour (BS, Notre-Dame Jamhour-Lebanon; MD, St. Joseph University, Beirut-Lebanon) is originally from Lebanon. He moved to the United States in 1996 where he completed his internal medicine and gastroenterology fellowship at the University of Robert Wood Johnson's Cooper hospital in Camden, NJ. He is a clinical Associate Professor at the University of North Dakota School of Medicine and Health Sciences, the Governor for the North Dakota American College of Physicians, and a past president of the North Dakota Medical Association. He owns his private clinic in Fargo, ND and provides care for our veterans in the Fargo VA healthcare system. Fadel's primary interest, besides his family and world history, is the field of gastrointestinal functional disorders and microbiome health.

Peter Schultz (BA, Concordia College; MA, Vanderbilt University; PhD, University of Athens) is an archaeologist and conservationist. He's the current Executive Director of the Longspur Prairie Fund. Peter has held advanced fellowships from the Fulbright Foundation, the National Endowment for the Humanities, the A.G. Leventis Foundation, the American School of Classical Studies, among many others. His research interests include ancient Greek art and literature, the philosophy of mind, and regenerative agriculture. His most recent academic books are *Artists and Artistic Production in Ancient Greece* (Cambridge University Press, 2017) and *The Thymele at Epidauros. Healing, Space, and Musical Performance in Late Classical Greece* (Theran Press, 2017).

William Schultz (BA, Concordia College; MA, Minnesota School of Professional Psychology) is a psychotherapist in private practice, a mental health researcher, and an OCD survivor. William's private practice is focused on helping individuals heal from anxious and depressive dynamics. His research centers on the dangers and shortcomings of biogenetic etiologies of mental disorders. William's work has been published in numerous peer-reviewed journals and forms a basis for developing internationally recognized competency standards for clinicians treating OCD. His most recent book is *Mental Health: Biology, Agency, Meaning* (Theran Press, 2019).

Noreen Thomas (BS, NDSU) and her family live on a 1200-acre farm — the world-renowned Doubting Thomas Farms — an operation that has been in continuous business for six generations. Established in 1878 along the Buffalo River near Moorhead, MN, the family farm grows organic blue corn, rye, wheat, hay, soybeans, peas, barley, oats, perennial flax, and perennial sunflowers. Find them right here at: www.doubtingthomasfarms.com. Noreen took a BS from NDSU in food nutrition, microbiology, and chemistry. She's always been interested in the intersection of nutrient-dense foods, agriculture, and the environment. Noreen was the first female farmer and the first organic farmer to receive the Siehl Prize for Excellence in Agriculture. She's also been awarded a Disney National Community Award, the American Heart Association's Creative Excellence Award, and has been featured on the Food Network and in numerous scientific publications.

❧ ACKNOWLEDGMENTS

First, we collectively acknowledge that, here in the Midwest, we live and eat from the traditional lands of the Nu'eta (Mandan), Hidatsa, Sanish (Arikara), Lakota/Dakota, and Anishinabe/Ojibwe/Chippewa people. If you live in Minnesota, then you may live on lands that were of the eleven American Indian tribes that have borders within the state. It is through the removal, relocation, forced assimilation, unkept treaty obligations, and other policies of the United States and state governments that the health and lives of Indigenous people have been damaged. It is Indigenous people who experience some of the highest rates of food insecurity throughout the Midwest. With this in mind, let us work together in a just way to acknowledge and repair what we can of this harm. Let us also acknowledge the resilience and creativity of people working in food and agriculture, and work toward true justice in land and food access. Let us respect and learn from Indigenous people who have always recognized the true connections between a healthy Earth, healthy lands, and healthy people.

Additionally, David Clardy would like to acknowledge and thank his organizations, the American College of Cardiology, the American Heart Association, and the American Society of Preventive Cardiology who—through their conferences, research, and publications—have formed the basis of his scientific knowledge of heart health. He would also like to thank his colleagues at Sanford Heart for the inspiration and support in allowing him to pursue his interest in heart healthy living. Megan Myrdal would like to thank her fellow teammates at Food of the North, Gia Rassier and Annie Wood, for their brilliance, passion, and dedication to our work; it's truly an honor and joy to work with you both. She would also like to thank her grandmother, Rosemarie Myrdal, for unknowingly inspiring her life journey of exploring ways to support the food and farming culture of our region. Fadel Nammour would like to thank his co-authors for making this book a reality. Peter Schultz would like to express his gratitude to Eugene Ladopoulos, Olga Palagia, and Giannis Ladopoulos for their endless kindness; in many ways, this project is their own. Noreen Thomas would like to thank Steve Zwinger, Dipayan Sarkar, and her farm family that always keep her coffee and heart warm. The entire Midwest Mediterranean team would like to offer a special thanks to Karen Ehrens for her gracious inputs and for challenging us to think critically about food accessibility, equity, and justice.

Finally, the publication of this book would not have been possible without the support of the Theran Press and its advisory board; the authors are happy to thank the Press for its generosity, positivity, and good humor.

The shared meal elevates eating from a mechanical process of fueling the body to a ritual of family and community, from mere animal biology to an act of culture.

— Michael Pollan

When you have the best and tastiest ingredients, you can cook very simply and the food will be extraordinary because it tastes like what it is.

— Alice Waters

To eat is a necessity – but to eat intelligently is an art.

— François de La Rochefoucauld

# INTRODUCTION
MEDITERRANEAN EATING IN THE AMERICAN MIDWEST

A *Mediterranean*-style diet that's grounded in the upper-*Midwest*?

You might be asking ... *why*?

Why are we talking about food from areas like Italy, Turkey, Lebanon, North Africa, and Greece in the High Plains of North America? Why would we ever look to places thousands of miles from our home — to places with climates, cultures, foods, agriculture landscapes, and cuisines — that so dramatically differ from our own?

Why would we look *there* to learn how to eat *here*?

Well, there are several profoundly important reasons, as you'll read throughout this book, but first there's a story — a story centered around exceptionally delicious extra-virgin olive oil.

In 1997, Peter Schultz, my co-editor and contributing author for *Midwest Mediterranean,* began his PhD in Greece. There, he met Eugene Ladopoulos, a Greek farmer and olive oil producer, and discovered Mr. Ladopoulos's "liquid gold" — aka the famous and wildly popular Mistra Estates Extra-Virgin Olive Oil.

At that time, Mr. Ladopoulos's family had owned land and olive trees near ancient Sparta for generations, but that year was his first attempt to sell his oil in America. Peter was astonished by the flavor and quality of this oil, as well as the exceptional care Eugene took of his trees and his lands. Over time, Peter joined Eugene on his mission to bring this liquid gold to America — founding Peter Schultz, Importer and delivering this world-class product to friends across the upper Midwest.

Fast forward to 2019.

Peter and I were working together on several projects centered on "cultivating sustainable habits"—a phrase we use often to describe our work—and he asked if I would partner to create a recipe using Mistra Estates Extra-Virgin Olive Oil featuring locally grown, Midwest ingredients. I agreed and created Midwest Mediterranean Bean Salad (p. 61-62)—a dish featuring seasonal kale, cucumbers, tomatoes, onions, and herbs from our local Red River Market, plus dry-edible beans that are grown in abundance across the upper Midwest, paired with classic Mediterranean ingredients—olive oil, balsamic vinegar, feta cheese, and olives. It isn't a complicated, fancy, or high-end recipe—it is simple home cooking! And—not to brag—it was freaking *delicious*! Everyone who's tasted it has been blown away by how incredible Midwest grown ingredients can taste when paired with key foods and flavors of the Mediterranean.

That was the idea—the idea that local, healthy, Midwest-grown ingredients could be brilliantly paired with the techniques, foods, and recipes of the Mediterranean for both flavor and health—that sparked something. Peter and I both saw it. We both *tasted* it! There was something truly magical there!

And, just like that, *Midwest Mediterranean* was born.

Now, I knew that I could speak with knowledge on dietary issues and that Peter could talk about olive oil for—literally—days on end.

But that wasn't enough.

To continue to fan the flames of this idea, to continue to crystallize our message, we realized that we needed a wider range of experts. This kind of project wasn't just about nutrition or ingredients, it was also about human biology, local ecologies, fair agriculture, deep sustainability, a passion for truly great living—and so much more! Peter and I were enthusiastic, but we clearly needed to add more experts to the team.

Over the next several months, we asked a number of brilliant advocates for this way of eating—and living!—to join our journey. The first was David Clardy, renowned cardiologist and a dear friend of Peter's, who has traveled to Greece, who has personally cooked and eaten like a Midwest Mediterranean for decades, and who has some first-hand insights into the connection between the Mediterranean diet and heart health. Next came Fadel Nammour, world-famous gastroenterologist, whose brilliant research on gut health and our microbiome are profoundly shaping how Midwesterners think about the impact of diet on health and wellbeing. My dear friend, Noreen Thomas, was next—a philosopher farmer whose commitment to growing foods for health and flavor has inspired cooks and eaters across the Midwest and beyond. Finally, Peter's brother, acclaimed therapist and scholar William Schultz, also joined the team. The spirit of authentic community collaboration was infectious and has guided every aspect of this little book's composition.

Indeed, to close this introduction, it might be worthwhile to reflect a moment on this notion of what a real Midwest Mediterranean *community* means for us. This book was written by a team of Midwesterners from diverse backgrounds, a team that shares a zeal for healthy food, healthy lives, and healthy souls. This book dips into history, agriculture, biology, philosophy, botany, ingredients, lifestyle, and more. This book is also packed with a collection of amazing Midwest Mediterranean recipes created by, yet again, even more community collaborators: chefs and home cooks from across the Midwest and the Mediterranean who are truly passionate about this diet and this way of life. My point is that this little book that you now hold in your hands isn't just a "cookbook." It's not just a "health book" or a "diet book," either. And it's certainly not just a "book about food." This project is more like an amazing smorgasbord of principles and particulars—a kind of eclectic community table that we've all helped create, a table at which we can all sit, share, learn, and enjoy. In this case, the table is loaded with some truly life-changing ideas that we feel deserve the widest possible audience. In that spirit, we're honored to offer this book to the community that gave it life, with the hopes that we can all continue to enjoy learning and thinking about the food, the people, the recipes, and the stories that connect us to this amazing way of eating and living.

— Megan Myrdal

Midwest Mediterranean

CHAPTER ONE
A BRIEF PREHISTORY
OF THE MEDITERRANEAN DIET

🌿 PETER SCHULTZ, PHD

The people cooking and eating around the Mediterranean Sea cook and eat many different kinds of food. And yet, these different foods share many common characteristics. You're going to be learning about some of these traits in the next five chapters of this book. Here, in Chapter One, I'm going to talk about the history of the Mediterranean diet and the early use of its constituent ingredients. A basic understanding of the ancient origins of these foods seems like a fun and interesting way to begin to appreciate the traditions and benefits of this amazing way of eating.

The term "Mediterranean diet" and its breakthrough into the public eye are the results of the work of Dr. Ancel Keys (1904-2004). Keys was a physiologist from Minnesota. He was also the first scientist to document the extraordinarily low incidence of cardiovascular disease in the communities of the Mediterranean when compared to other areas of the world. Keys believed that diet was the primary determining factor in this comparison. Keys' famous study, published in 1970, was the result of research that he and his team carried out over ten years on 12,000+ men from seven countries: Finland, Greece, Italy, Japan, Holland, the United States, and Yugoslavia. The results of this study are now well known. Of these seven nations, the United States and Finland had the highest animal product consumption, the highest saturated fat intake, and—by far—the highest percentage of deaths from cardiovascular diseases. Japan, Italy, and Greece showed the exact opposite trends. Keys' "Seven Countries Study" marked the beginning of serious research into the benefits of the Mediterranean diet. This research resulted in a series of scientific conclusions that have been confirmed over the last fifty years. The Mediterranean diet has numerous, documented benefits. These benefits include the primary and secondary prevention of cardiovascular diseases, obesity, type 2 diabetes, metabolic disorders, numerous forms of cancer, and a host of neurodegenerative diseases, as well as many, many other benefits. David, Megan, and Fadel's chapters will all give detailed summaries of recent research from their specific fields that confirm this well-known and long-standing general consensus: *The Mediterranean diet is good for you.*

But how long have people been eating like this?

Before getting into some answers to that question, it's worth thinking about the ancient Greek word from which the word "diet" is derived. In ancient Greek, the word is δίαιτᾰ. It changes only slightly in modern Greek to δίαιτα. It is transliterated *díaita* and pronounced with the stress on the first syllable, like this: DEE-ai-ta. This is worth noting because in both ancient and modern usage the word díaita does not just mean "diet." Rather, as you may have already guessed, the word means something a bit more, something along the lines of "way of life," or "mode of existence," or "lifestyle." The ancient Greek verb from which this word comes — διαιτάω, to "manage," or to "handle" — further shows how closely connected this word is with "an approach to living." This is an important point. The Mediterranean lifestyle isn't just about what food to eat. It's also about long walks on the beach, relaxing conversations with friends, long naps in the afternoons, passionate celebrations in the evening, and a general zest for living fully and in the moment. While the biological benefits derived from the Mediterranean diet are well documented and important, we'd do well to remember that holistic health includes the mind, body, and soul.

It's also important to note that this way of eating is most definitely *not* a "fad diet." Quite the opposite. We have solid archaeological evidence for human consumption of the Mediterranean diet's key ingredients going back to the Neolithic period and earlier. We also have nearly fifty years of rigorous scientific study documenting the diet's efficacy and advantages. Compare this, for example, to the—now debunked—"Paleo diet," a trademarked branding exercise supported by zero archaeological research and no long-term clinical studies of its claimed benefits. (There has been some recent work on *risks* of the "Paleo diet," but that's a topic for another time.) I mention this only to make clear that the foods and practices associated with the Mediterranean diet are truly ancient and truly beneficial. The Mediterranean diet is not a "trendy internet craze." It's a way of eating that has been practiced since the beginnings of human civilization.

In terms of the diet's history, let's start by thinking about ancient whole grains. The remains of burnt grain tend to survive forever when buried, so there's a good amount of archaeological evidence for eating whole grains in antiquity. For example, barley was being cultivated on the northern edges of the Mediterranean over 9,000 years ago. Another ancient grain that's native to the eastern Mediterranean and the Mediterranean coast of North Africa is *freekeh*, pronounced like this: FREE-kah. Freekeh, also known as *farik*, is a roasted green wheat. The word is Arabic and means "what is rubbed," referring to the rubbing technique necessary for processing. The grain was called *carmel* in ancient Hebrew and was eaten by the ancient Israelites; it's mentioned in the Bible, Leviticus 23:14, as a part of the first fruits offering that Jewish worshipers brought to the Temple in Jerusalem each year for the holiday of Shavuot.

Modern wheat (*Triticum aestivum*) has its genetic roots in three varieties of grain that were used in the ancient Mediterranean and Near East for at least ten millennia. These three ancient types are now known as *spelt, einkorn,* and *emmer.* Spelt was originally cultivated in what's now Iran and in southeastern Europe. It was a staple of its day and one of the very first wheats used to make bread. Spelt was called *zeiá* by the ancient Greeks and was said to be a gift from the goddess Demeter. The earliest evidence for the cultivation and consumption of spelt comes from the northern Mediterranean and the coasts of the Black Sea; its use seems to date to at least 10,000 years before the present. Einkorn was used even earlier. It's a tough grain that was grown in Europe since

Mesolithic times — over 15,000-5,000 years ago. There's solid archaeological evidence of einkorn farming in both the Karaca Dag Mountains of southeast Turkey, and in ancient Jericho. Both examples date to at least 9,000 B.C.E. The use of emmer might be even older. It was an original staple of farming in the Levant and was also eaten by ancient people living in the Middle East and Egypt. Grains of wild emmer have been discovered at the archaeological site of Ohalo, Israel and have been dated to 17,000 B.C.E. The term "ancient grains" isn't a marketing tool. These staples of the Mediterranean diet are truly primordial.

Lentils, a key legume in the Mediterranean diet, also have an ancient pedigree. Thought to have originated in the ancient Near East and Mediterranean, lentils have been a source of protein and fiber for humans since prehistoric times. They're the oldest known pulse crop (a crop harvested solely for dried seed) and one of humanity's earliest domesticated crops. The word *lentil* comes from the Latin *lens* because of its shape; the sophisticated double-convex optic lens took its name from the humble lentil. The physical remains of lentils have been found on archeological digs on the banks of the Euphrates River dating back to 8,000 B.C.E. and there's evidence for all ancient Mediterranean cultures — the Egyptians, Greeks, Romans, and Hebrews — eating this legume. Like freekeh, lentils are also mentioned in the Bible. One example is in the book of Genesis (25:29-34) and the story of Esau, who gave up his birthright for a loaf of bread and a bowl of lentils. In 2017, Dr. Valentina Caracuta (Max Planck-Weizmann Center for Integrative Archaeology and Anthropology, Rehovot, Israel) conducted an archaeological study of ancient lentil residue using gas chromatography-mass spectrometry (GC-MS) at the prehistoric site of Ahihud in Israel. She determined that the farming of lentils had been practiced in the southern Levant for at least 12,000 years.

Fish and seafood provide key sources of healthy protein for Mediterranean diets. Like ancient grains, these foods seem to have been consumed by Mediterraneans since the most ancient of times. It's been pretty well-known since the early 1970s that early humans fished on the open sea since at least 12,000 B.C.E. Recently, however, Dr. Sue O'Connor (Australian National University, Canberra) discovered evidence of prehistoric fishing gear in a cave located on East Timor. This excavation uncovered bone fishing hooks that date to about 42,000 years ago, making these fishhooks some of the earliest physical evidence for fishing in the world. Closer to the Mediterranean proper, solid evidence has now emerged that both human and contemporary Neanderthal populations were fishing and eating seafood *very* early indeed. New dietary analyses of a Neanderthal site in Figueira Brava, south of Lisbon, Portugal, conducted by Dr. João Zilhão (University of Barcelona), shows that the Neanderthals had an eclectic diet — but that they ate mostly seafood. Dr. Zilhão's site has been dated between 106,000-86,000 years old. The Mediterranean Sea itself provides even earlier archaeological evidence for the consumption of fish. In 2005, Dr. Mary Stiner (University of Arizona, Tucson) published her book *The Faunas of Hayonim Cave: A 200,000-Year Record of Paleolithic Diet, Demography, and Society.* This incredibly detailed study conclusively shows that early Mediterraneans, specifically those living on the western coast of modern Israel, systematically consumed fish as a key staple in their diets. Some of her evidence from Hayonim Cave is over 200,000(!) years old. This data represents some of the earliest ever for prehistoric human eating habits in the Mediterranean basin.

What about olive oil? How long have people been using this staple of the Mediterranean diet? Nuclear magnetic resonance (NMR) and gas chromatography-mass spectrometry (GC-MS) allow archaeologists to identify a number of different natural substances preserved in archaeological environments. Olive oil is a natural subject for this work. In 2018, for example, Dr. David Tanusis (University of South Florida) presented a protocol for detecting natural compounds within amorphous organic residues discovered inside the pores of prehistoric pottery. His study was based on pots excavated in the Middle Bronze Age settlement of Castelluccio in southern Italy. These pottery remains can be firmly dated to the end of the 3rd and the beginning of the 2nd millennium B.C.E. What did Dr. Tanusis discover was originally held in these ancient pots? Olive oil. In other words, sometime around 2,100-1,900 B.C.E., early "Italians" were using large quantities of olive oil in their meals. Of course, olive oil was also used for many other purposes in the ancient world, but the presence of identified residue in both storage- and dining-ware proves beyond all doubt that these folks were eating olive oil — and a lot of it. In a similar fashion, Dr. Andrew Koh (MIT) and my colleague, Dr. Paul Betancourt (Professor Emeritus, Temple University), showed that the nine *pithoi* — large pots — excavated from the small hilltop site of "Aphrodite's Kepahli" in eastern Crete contained both wine and olive oil. This is important since the occupation of this site can be firmly dated to the Early Bronze Age, ca. 3,200-2,700 B.C.E., a full millennium *earlier* than the Italian evidence at Castelluccio. But even these remains seem modern when compared to the evidence that Dr. Dvory Namdar (Israel Institute of Technology) discovered at his excavations at the Giv' at Rabi excavations, just east of the Sea of Galilee. There, ancient pottery from many of the site's levels were subjected to organic residue analysis study and then analyzed using GC-MS. Olive oil was one of the most common organic residues detected in the vessels. This important find sheds important new light on the use of olives in the southern Levant as well as on the large-scale production and consumption of olive oil in Late Neolithic times. But here's why this really matters: The Giv' at Rabi settlement was inhabited between 6,000-5,000 B.C.E., the Late Neolithic period — over 8,000 years ago. The use of olive oil is thus documented before the dawn of the Bronze Age.

Now, does any of this prove that the Mediterranean diet is good for you, or that we should all start eating like ancient Greeks, or that Mediterranean food tastes good?

Not at all.

What it does show is that people have been enjoying this kind of cuisine since before the dawn of civilization. Indeed, the Mediterranean diet can rightfully be considered one of the first "diets"—ever. So, if you're looking for a diet that's good for the mind, body, and soul, then this is the one. And if you're looking for a diet that stands at the end of one of the most consistent food traditions in human history, then look no further.

Enjoy!

Chapter Two
Healthy Eating with Foods & Flavors
of the Mediterranean

Megan Myrdal, MS, RDN

In the northern tier of the Midwest, we have many things to be proud of. Sadly, good health is not one of them. Despite years of trying to promote well-being and to reduce chronic diseases, the statistics on nearly every front continue to worsen. We eat too much of what we should not — highly processed, calorically dense foods — and too little of what we should — nutrient-rich fruits and vegetables. We are sicker, heavier, and for many — living shorter lives.

Diet has been recognized as one of the most significant lifestyle factors that impacts our overall health. As a registered dietitian, I know that almost any diet will work, as long as it's followed long term. Unfortunately, the restrictive nature of most diets — and the fact that they lack delicious flavors — leaves most followers feeling deprived and thus makes the diet unsustainable. Sure, most people are able to follow a restrictive diet for 3-6 months, but within a year they've regained most, if not all, of their weight back. Fortunately, unlike many other diets, the Mediterranean diet isn't a "diet" at all.

Rather, it's a *lifestyle*.

The Mediterranean diet is composed of the cuisine that the people of the Mediterranean have been eating and enjoying for millennia. It gained widespread scientific interest in the 1970s, when medical researchers noticed that people who lived in these countries had lower instances of chronic diseases and were living longer, healthier lives. The research since that discovery has blossomed to create a compelling case for why every person should eat like a Mediterranean!

In this chapter, I'll discuss the various foods that are signature to the Mediterranean diet as well as what nutrients are found in those foods that nourish our bodies. Further, we'll look at many of the Mediterranean diet foods that are grown in abundance here in the North and how we can incorporate these foods into a local "Midwest Mediterranean" cuisine. In addition, it's important to acknowledge that there are some who may find it difficult to follow a Midwest Mediterranean diet due to financial constraints. I'll share some tips to make easy, delicious Midwest Mediterranean meals available to those on a strict budget. And finally, I'll share eight easy ways that can help you make the switch from the classic Midwest diet to the Midwest Mediterranean diet.

What is the Mediterranean Diet?
The traditional Mediterranean diet is based on foods available in countries that border the Mediterranean Sea. The foundation of this healthy diet includes:

- **An abundance of plant foods including whole grains, legumes (beans, peas, lentils, and chickpeas), fruits, vegetables, and nuts—ideally those that are minimally processed and locally grown**
- **Olive oil as the principal fat**
- **Cheese and yogurt—consumed in low to moderate amounts daily**
- **Fish and poultry—consumed in low to moderate amounts a few times a week**
- **Wine—consumed in low to moderate amounts, usually with meals**
- **Infrequent consumption of red meat, refined grains, and sweets**

It's important to note that no one food will guarantee good health. When you read about the Mediterranean diet, a lot of attention goes to a small group of foods—typically red wine and extra-virgin olive oil. While these foods are important parts of the diet, a healthy diet takes the total diet into account; the healthiest

10

Mediterranean diets include a wide variety of all the foods listed above, eaten in moderate portions. However, it's nice to know a little about the core foods, what benefits they provide, and how we can make the healthiest choices. Let's take a closer look at a few of these foods—whole grains, legumes, fruits and vegetables, nuts and seeds, and extra-virgin olive oil—which are key tenets of the Mediterranean diet.

Whole Grains
A key principle of the Mediterranean diet is to enjoy more whole grains. When you eat whole grains, you receive the most nutritional benefit from the grain—from micronutrients and fiber—and have the lowest glycemic index, a term that describes how quickly our blood sugars rise when we eat a certain food.

All grains start as whole grains, but many are modified through refining and processing. The "whole" grain, as it is grown in the field, is the entire seed of the plant and is made up of three edible parts: the bran, the germ, and the endosperm. When a grain is refined, parts of the grain are removed (bran and germ), leaving us with just the starch-rich endosperm. Losing the bran and germ denies your body the good nutrition the whole grain provides. In addition, the act of mechanical processing does the work our bodies would normally have to do in digestion. Processing is essentially grinding or milling a grain into smaller, finer particles (aka flour). The more finely milled a grain is, the more quickly our body is able to digest it. A key principle of the Mediterranean diet is an emphasis on whole grains; grains in their whole form leave more work for the body to do, creating slower digestion and a far lower blood glucose response.

There are many delicious whole grains to enjoy, including: barley, buckwheat, bulgur, couscous, durum, farro, freekeh, millet, oats, polenta, rice, and wheat berries. While not all are native to the Midwest, our region of the world produces many grains in abundance, including: barley, oats, millet, and wheat. Furthermore, many farmers in our region are diversifying into ancient grains like emmer and spelt. All of these grains

11

can be incorporated into a delicious and nutritious Midwest Mediterranean diet.

Legumes
Legume is a term that encompasses beans, peas, chickpeas, and lentils. These foods are exceptionally nutritious and are enjoyed in abundance in the Mediterranean diet. As a source of plant-based protein, fiber, and other important nutrients, legumes provide significant nutritional and health benefits.

Perhaps you're starting to notice a pattern. The key foods emphasized in the Mediterranean diet are plant-based. While you can still enjoy animal products, you are encouraged to do so in smaller quantities. Legumes are a rich source of plant-based protein—a ½ cup serving of beans (cooked) has approximately 8 grams of protein, which is comparable to an ounce of meat (7 grams of protein) or an egg (6 grams of protein). The added bonus of legumes is that in addition to protein, you are also getting fiber not found in animal products. A diet rich in fiber is associated with many positive health outcomes including good digestion, improved blood glucose control, and a lower risk of chronic diseases. In Chapter Five and Six, you will read all about how the Mediterranean diet improves cardiovascular and gastrointestinal health. Fiber is a big contributor to those benefits!

Legumes are typically available in two forms—dried or canned. Dried legumes are exactly as they sound—dry. In order to enjoy, they need to be soaked in water and cooked (except lentils which cook relatively quickly from their dry form). Canned legumes have already been rehydrated and cooked. They simply need to be warmed through to enjoy or added directly to any recipe. One of the main differences between dried and canned legumes is the amount of sodium they contain. For example, a ½ cup serving of pinto beans cooked from dry beans is virtually sodium free, while a ½ cup serving of canned pinto beans contains approximately 200 milligrams of sodium. You can drain and rinse canned beans to remove about 40% of the sodium.

In the upper Midwest, we grow legumes in abundance. The common varieties enjoyed in Mediterranean cuisines are cannellini, chickpeas, fava, green, kidney, lentils, and split peas. In the upper Midwest, we also grow pinto, black, navy, great northern, red, pink, and cranberry beans, in addition to chickpeas, kidney beans, and lentils. All forms of legumes are good for your health. The rule of thumb about legumes is: Eat more!

Fruits & Vegetables

When it comes to fruits and vegetables, like legumes, the key takeaway from the Mediterranean diet is to eat more. Fruits and vegetables—loaded with antioxidants, key nutrients, and fiber—are the building blocks for good health.

In the Mediterranean diet, key fruits include apples, apricots, cherries, clementines, dates, figs, grapefruit, grapes, lemons, melons, nectarines, oranges, peaches, pears, pomegranates, strawberries, and tangerines. For vegetables, Mediterraneans enjoy a vast assortment: artichokes, arugula, beets, broccoli, brussels sprouts, cabbage, carrots, celery, celeriac, chicory, collards, cucumbers, dandelion greens, eggplant, fennel, kale, leeks, lettuce, mache, mushrooms, mustard greens, nettles, okra, onions, peas, peppers, potatoes, pumpkins, purslane, radishes, rutabaga, scallions, shallots, spinach, sweet potatoes, tomatoes, turnips, and zucchini.

In the upper Midwest, we grow fruits and vegetables in abundance, but our growing season is too short and our winters too harsh for certain fruits—especially citrus. However, the list of what we can't grow is much shorter than what we can. In the producing months, check out your local farmers market to enjoy the seasonal abundance. And if you have a garden, eat what you can in season and use preservation techniques like canning, pickling, freezing, fermentation, and dehydrating to extend the life of your food into the winter months. Your local Extension Office has great resources on how to properly preserve garden produce that's specific to your region, as well as the National

Center for Home Food Preservation. You can never have enough canned tomatoes for your Midwest Mediterranean diet!

Nuts & Seeds
Nuts and seeds have played an important role in the Mediterranean diet for centuries. A flavorful little package that contains healthy fats, fiber, protein, and other nutrients—just a small handful can add a lot of great nutrition and flavor to your meal. Though the specific nutrients vary between different nuts and seeds, most contain a good profile of mono- and polyunsaturated fat. When these types of fats are eaten in moderation, they can provide positive health outcomes, like a reduced risk of cardiovascular disease.

Nuts and seeds traditional to the Mediterranean diet include almonds, cashews, hazelnuts, pine nuts, pistachios, sesame seeds (tahini), and walnuts. These foods not only add good nutrition to your menu, but also exceptional flavor and crunch. Tossing in a handful of toasted walnuts will liven up any salad—just remember to lightly toast them to bring out their flavor!

While our northern Midwestern climate is not ideal for growing nuts, we are a top producer of sunflower seeds, which make a great snack, salad topper, or a nice nut butter.

Extra-Virgin Olive Oil
One of the most important, distinguishing aspects of the Mediterranean diet is its emphasis on healthy fats, namely cold-pressed, extra-virgin olive oil. Extra-virgin olive oil is rich in monounsaturated fat. Using extra-virgin olive oil to replace saturated sources of fat (like butter) has been associated with improved blood cholesterol levels, raising good cholesterol (HDL) and lowering bad cholesterol (LDL). In addition to being rich in unsaturated fat, extra-virgin olive oil has antioxidants that offer bodily benefits beyond improved cholesterol.

Research into the Mediterranean diet was key in dispelling the myth that a healthy diet needs to be low in fat. The Mediterranean diet allows for a generous portion of daily calories to come from fat—35-45%—emphasizing that those fats should come from healthy sources. In other words, even when people follow a Mediterranean-style diet *high* in fat, they see improved cardiovascular health. You'll learn much more about this from Dr. Clardy in Chapter Five!

While olive oil is not native to the Midwest, there are ample sources of authentic, high quality, cold-pressed, extra-virgin olive oil available in local markets. It's important to remember that there's incredible variation in olive oil; it may be buttery and soft, spicy and sharp, or fruity and grassy. A preferred olive oil really comes down to personal preference and culinary application; most prefer a mild olive oil for general cooking, and something with a little more flavor punch for dressings or finishing a dish. You also want to make sure you're purchasing something of high quality. "Extra-virgin" is the highest designation of quality given to olive oil, meaning it's unrefined, chemical-free, never treated with heat, and free from other defects. It's also a good rule of thumb to purchase olive oil that comes from a single place and when possible, from a single producer. The language on the bottle can be tricky so read the fine print to ensure you get a single-origin, great-tasting olive oil! Peter has put together a wonderful buying guide to assist you with this at the back of the book.

A key thing to remember with both nuts and seeds and extra-virgin olive oil is that you should enjoy them regularly, but do so in moderation. Since they are both significant sources of fat, they are calorically dense foods. A tablespoon of olive oil has approximately 120 calories and a 1-ounce (¼ cup) serving of mixed nuts has about 170 calories. Incorporate these foods into your diet, but do so in moderation to maintain a healthy weight.

What About Budget?
Eating, especially eating healthily, on a limited budget is not easy. Some research has shown that the Mediterranean diet pattern can be more expensive for some consumers. The U.S. News and

World Reports ranked the Mediterranean Diet "#1 Best Diet Overall," but also described it as "moderately pricey."

The truth is that foods within a Midwest Mediterranean diet are found across a wide range of prices, from pretty expensive to dirt cheap. Sure, if you eat wild caught salmon with expensive cheese and wine for most meals, your food budget will reflect this. However, many of the signature foods of the Midwest Mediterranean diet are also some of the least expensive foods on the market—particularly whole grains and legumes! And bonus—these foods are grown in abundance across the upper Midwest! When you eat like a Mediterranean, you eat less of many foods that are more expensive, such as meat and highly processed foods, leaving more food budget to purchase the nutrient-rich Midwest Mediterranean ingredients.

It's important to acknowledge that price alone is not the only barrier people face to purchasing and enjoying healthful foods. There are many barriers that keep people from eating in a way that nourishes their bodies—some we can control and others we can't. Here, I hope to present some ways that people can make the Midwest Mediterranean diet more affordable, but we must acknowledge that many societal, political, and cultural changes are needed to provide everyone an opportunity eat healthily. While the focus of this book is more on the decisions we can make as individuals, I encourage everyone to learn more about the various government programs and efforts underway to make healthy, local, and well-grown food available to all.

MEGAN'S TIPS FOR EATING MIDWEST MEDITERRANEAN ON A BUDGET

1. Eat at home and cook from scratch.
This tip is by far the simplest, but also the most important. The more you cook and eat at home, the more money you'll save. The more you're cooking from scratch, the healthier your meals will be. Forbes Magazine compared 86 meals and how much it costs to

purchase the groceries for home cooking versus restaurant delivery. They found, on average, that it was five times more expensive to order restaurant delivery than cooking at home! Obviously, cooking meals at home takes more time, but you get a healthier product and you also get to control what goes into your recipe. If you see time spent in the kitchen as drudgery, try to change your perspective and see kitchen time as a learning opportunity. If you feel like your skills in the kitchen are subpar, attend a cooking class. If that's too expensive, watch a cooking video on YouTube! It's free and there's a lot of excellent, high-quality content from masterful chefs and cooks across the world; you can practice right along with them in your home kitchen at zero cost.

My two favorite pieces of advice to enhance your home cooking experience are (a) improve your knife skills and, (b) season as you cook. Improving your knife skills is one of the best ways to elevate your cooking experience, creating a more efficient, safe process, while also saving you money. (The more whole, intact food you buy, the less work you're paying someone else to do for you.) Next, taste and season as you cook. It is truly amazing what a little salt or acid at the right time can do for a dish. As a wise chef once told me: "If you're good to your ingredients, then they will be good to you."

2. Build a pantry.
With a well-stocked pantry, you can put together so many meals in a matter of minutes and you can do so on a pretty modest budget! Midwest Mediterranean pantry basics include a variety of grains (barley, oats, rice, wheat berries), beans & lentils (canned and dried), fruits & vegetables (fresh, frozen, and canned), flavorful condiments (olive oil, vinegar, herbs, spices), dairy (cheese, butter, milk, yogurt), and proteins (eggs, nuts and nut butters, tuna, salmon, and sardines). When you have funds and find pantry essentials on sale, stock up. Canned goods' shelf life is easily two years, if not longer, and dry goods like grains and beans are also good for more than a year. Herbs, spices, oils, and vinegars can be a little pricey, but try to reserve part of your food budget and purchase one or two of the more expensive pantry

items a week. These ingredients are key to bring out the signature Mediterranean flavors, and you only need to use a little. They'll go a long way!

3. Buy in bulk.
Buying food in larger quantities brings the prices down. Think about ingredients that you use very frequently in your kitchen, or ingredients that have a lot of versatility, and see if purchasing them in bulk makes sense for you and your family. Personally, I do a lot of purchasing in bulk because I appreciate the prices, I tend to use the same "base ingredients" in most of my meals, and I find the quality to be high. Items that I purchase in bulk that work well in my Midwest Mediterranean kitchen include olive oil, olives, lemons, garlic, vinegars, feta cheese, oat groats, beans, nuts (I store them in the freezer), and canned tomatoes. I use them frequently in many dishes, and when I compare the cost of buying them in smaller quantities, it's about $2/3$ of the price.

4. Shop seasonally.
When you buy what's in season, you buy foods that are at peak supply, which generally means that they are cheaper and tastier. Zucchini in the middle of winter might cost you $3 for a small squash, but people practically give them away at the end of summer. Every growing region is a little different so check out your local farmers market to know what's in season in your area, and if you are able, buy as much produce as you can from these local markets. The prices may be a little higher than traditional grocery stores, but the quality is typically very high and you are supporting your local farmers and local economy at the same time!

5. Don't waste food.
The average American household throws away about 25% of the food it purchases. For the average family of four, this comes out to $1,365-$2,275 a year! Simply not throwing away food could have a significant impact on a household's budget. Some strategies to reduce food waste: cut down on portion sizes by using smaller plates and bowls; plan meals and prepare grocery lists in advance;

inventory your fridge, freezer, and pantry before you go grocery shopping; remember that the expiration dates on foods are based on quality, not safety; make smaller, more frequent trips to the grocery store for perishable items like produce; and make sure that leftover food, whether from a restaurant or home, gets packaged and stored for later use.

8 Steps to Make the Shift to "Midwest Mediterranean"

Now that you've learned the basics of the Mediterranean diet, acquired a general understanding of why these foods enhance overall health, and learned about how this can all work on budget, let's talk about shifting the traditional Midwest diet into a Midwest *Mediterranean* diet.

1. Go vegetarian one meal a day.
Our typical Midwestern diet is very meat-centric. One of the most health-promoting aspects of the Mediterranean diet is that it is a plant-based diet. In traditional Mediterranean-style dining, meat is seen as a condiment instead of the star of the meal. Try using less meat and make one vegetarian meal a day. Choose from the wide variety of plant-based sources of protein listed above like beans, peas, lentils, nuts, and seeds. A wonderful option for a plant-based, versatile meal is a whole grain salad paired with a legume tossed with some fresh vegetables, herbs, and an extra-virgin-olive-oil-based vinaigrette. There are endless variations of this—and it's delicious and nutritious!

2. Switch out whatever fat you are using to extra-virgin olive oil.
As you've already read, olive oil really is a star in the Mediterranean diet and is the primary source of fat for this style of eating. Midwestern food culture is fairly butter-centric, and while you can still enjoy butter on occasion, making the switch to extra-virgin olive oil as your primary fat can have extraordinary benefits. Extra-virgin olive oil can be used beyond vinaigrettes— frying eggs, sautéing or roasting vegetables, and making delicious

spreads and dips. If you are wondering what to put on bread, try dipping it in olive oil with some sea salt, pepper, and dried herbs.

3. Eat fruit and nuts for snacks.
Instead of relying on packaged snacks, laden with sugar, salt, and fat, plan fruits and nuts for your go-to snack. Or better yet: Pair them together. A piece of fresh fruit provides healthy fiber and natural sugar to give you some oomph, and nuts provide the plant-based protein to sustain your energy. Keep seasonal, fresh fruit and nuts on hand for a go-to snack.

4. Add more vegetables to your meals.
It's easy, and fairly common, to go through a whole day eating the classic Midwestern-style diet with no vegetables, or very few. A bowl of cereal for breakfast, sandwich and chips for lunch, and a steak and potato for dinner. In order to maximize the benefits of the Midwest Mediterranean diet, we need to think about how we can get as many vegetables as possible into our menu every single day. For breakfast, consider an omelet filled with peppers, onions, mushrooms, and sautéed greens. For lunch, try a sandwich with vegetables and a plant-based spread like hummus. For dinner, cut the steak and potato in half and add two vegetable sides, like roasted carrots and broccoli. A key tip: Every time you eat, think "What vegetable can I enjoy with this meal?" and eat it!

5. Make whole grains your preferred grains—the more intact the better.
To reap the benefits of the Mediterranean diet, it's essential to try to eat as many whole foods as possible—including whole grains. If you're currently eating white bread, rice, or pasta, try switching to a whole grain alternative. It may not provide the same creamy sweetness you are accustomed to, but the whole grain version has more texture and usually a more complex, interesting flavor. If you regularly eat whole grain bread, try a bowl featuring those same sandwich ingredients, but instead of bread, use fully intact whole grains. Remember: the more intact the grain the better! Choose whole grains like farro, barley, or oat berries (you'll learn more about these from Noreen in Chapter Three). If you're eating

a processed grain (like bread or pasta), choose the whole grain option.

6. Rethink the hotdish.
Hotdish is one of the most signature Midwest dishes, and typically features a refined grain, meat, some type of salty, fatty sauce, and possibly a small number of vegetables. Instead of using a refined grain like white pasta or rice, try a whole grain like quinoa or brown rice to increase the nutrition and fiber of your dish. Most classic Midwest hotdishes feature ground beef, and while a little meat is okay, a big emphasis of Midwest Mediterranean is looking for other sources of protein. Try using dried or canned beans, canned fish, or chicken in your hotdish. Get creative with the vegetables and make a goal to have at least two different vegetables in every hotdish. Finally, try making a homemade sauce (preferably one with extra-virgin olive oil) so you can control the salt and fat.

7. Eat more legumes.
With all the nutrition and health benefits, at just pennies a serving, legumes are a great addition to all Midwest Mediterranean meals and should be enjoyed daily. Legumes make a great addition to breakfast egg dishes like bakes, quiches, frittatas, or scrambles. They are also a wonderful way to enhance salads, sandwiches, pastas, or wraps. Furthermore, every pot of soup deserves a legume. A classic Mediterranean soup, Tuscan Ribollita, features cannellini beans, day-old bread, kale, extra-virgin olive oil, and inexpensive vegetables like carrots, celery, and onions. It's as simple as it is delicious!

8. Use herbs & spices to add signature flavors of the Mediterranean.
Herbs and spices are an important way to create the signature flavors of the Mediterranean right in your home kitchen. Classic herbs and spices from this region include anise, basil, bay leaf, chiles, clove, cumin, fennel, garlic, lavender, marjoram, mint, oregano, parsley, pepper, rosemary, sage, sumac, tarragon, and thyme. Use these herbs and spices in various combinations to

create signature Mediterranean flavors. To enjoy fresh herbs year-round, keep them in a well-lit area indoors to snip and enjoy as needed. To keep your store-bought spices fresh, make sure you rotate them regularly in your pantry, or keep them in your freezer to extend the shelf life.

CHAPTER THREE
FARMING FOR FLAVOR
IN THE UPPER MIDWEST

NOREEN THOMAS

As farmers in the upper Midwest, my family and I know firsthand the challenges and rewards of producing food in our place — a place with soils rich enough to grow almost anything, but a climate and latitude that only allows food to grow for 3-4 months a year. And as organic farmers, we take tremendous pride in the quality of the food we produce — exceptional nutrition, great flavor, and no pesticide use, as well as in knowing that we will leave the ground it came from as good, if not better, than when we started working it. A ground and soil that is amongst the richest in the world. We take pride in knowing that the farm we leave to the next generation will be healthy and sustainable.

We farm in the wheat lands of the Red River Valley, part of the breadbasket of America. In recent decades, many acres of this once-diversified grain land have been consumed by two crops — corn and soybeans. Our family farm, Doubting Thomas Farm, has not followed this trend. Instead, we have stayed committed to producing organic crops, including many grains that are Mediterranean diet staples. One crop that our farm specializes in is oats. I'd like to share a little about this particular grain: How oats are grown on our farm, what nutrition research has shown about the compounds in oats that promote good health, and how my family enjoys them as part of our Midwest Mediterranean diet. As Megan noted in the previous chapter, no single food will produce superior health — despite the "superfood" diet culture we live in today. Nevertheless, I hope this chapter will give you a sense of the tremendous value found in oats, as well as all the other amazing grains produced in the north.

The Way Things "Oat" To Be

Human cultures have been eating and enjoying oats for millennia. This history has left us with a multitude of recipes, including everything from the most primitive oat mash, to fall apple crisp treats, to fresh roasted pumpkin seed granola, to delicate berry-and-oat scones, to much—much!—more. While oats have a rich history in connection to our health and our ecosystems, they were once thought to be a "nuisance" or a "weed." We now know that oats are, in fact, one of our most important and beneficial grains.

Steve Zwinger, an agronomist at North Dakota State University, has long argued that oats are good for the soil, and adding oats to a crop rotation can add superb positive biomass and improve soil health. Our family has been farming in the Red River Valley since 1878, and I can say with confidence that oats have been an asset to our land and ecosystem. Even looking at an oat is a gorgeous picture in and of itself: Oat stems hanging in the field with their kernels arched and dangling right before harvest look much like little lanterns hanging on a grain stock.

As a farmer, I love knowing that what we're growing is good for our planet, good for our bodies, and good for our souls—exactly what we all want from a local, regenerative, healthy food. Oat plants are hearty and grow well in our area with our cool climate and our long growing days in the summer. Most important in the context of this little book, of course: Oats can play a positive and prominent role in a "Midwest Mediterranean" diet.

With regard to our bodies and the specific nutritional connection between oats and the dietary goals of Midwest Mediterranean cooking, the research around oats and their impact on health is strong.

One of the most well-known nutritional aspects of oats is that they are a rich source of fiber. A 100-gram serving (about 1 cup) of dry oats contains about 10 grams of dietary fiber, 8.5 grams of insoluble fiber, 4.2 g of soluble fiber, and 8.6 grams of beta glucan. Research suggests that just 3 grams of beta glucan a day can reduce your risk of heart disease by reducing blood cholesterol levels.

You might not think of protein when you think of oats, but it can be surprisingly high, which is a win for both vegetarians and vegans. However, measuring and growing "for protein" can be tricky as the protein levels of a grain depend on multiple factors such as soil type, oat type, and the growing conditions. That said, some protein levels we've seen with oats grown on our family farm measure over 12% of the USDA recommended daily allowance!

There are also important phenolic compounds and flavonoids found in oats, like catechin (also common in green tea), that are significant for improving human health and wellness. The catechin found in our oats is a potent antioxidant that may provide numerous health benefits such as cell protection and relief for inflammatory bowel disease. Oats with high catechin content may also help manage chronic diseases like type 2 diabetes, cardiovascular disease, and gut health complications.

A study out of North Dakota State University (NDSU) compared nutritional qualities and potential anti-diabetic and gut health benefits between whole grain oats and processed oats (Khalaf, 2018). This study found that whole grain oats are rich in phenolic bio-actives, as well as other dietary antioxidants, both of which help to control blood sugars. Additionally, whole grain oat extracts may support a healthy gut microbiome. In other words: Control bacterial pathogens and nourish the "good guys" of the human gut microbe world, which can help guard against ulcer causing bacteria, *Helicobacter pylori*, and other unwanted gut pathogens. Most importantly, the results of this study suggest that whole grain oats—like those that we grow here in the Red River Valley— have a much higher nutritional quality and health advantage than standard processed oats. This is a critical distinction.

In another NDSU study, researchers Eyada Khalaf, Dipayan Sarkar, and Kalidas Shetty showed that oats seem to have naturally occurring bioactive compounds that exhibit high antioxidant properties, similar to antioxidant rich grains and fruits. These antioxidants may naturally help to reduce inflammation and protect against metabolic breakdowns in humans.

Due to their superior bioactive profile, dietary fiber composition, and well-documented health benefits, oats — especially organic oats — are an inexpensive and natural dietary addition. The nutrients found in our locally grown organic oats, and the health benefits they provide, are entirely congruous with the well-known benefits of a Mediterranean diet.

While the health benefits of oats are documented and important, by far the most significant aspect of our oats is the *taste*. Local artisan farmers, like us here in the Red River Valley, actually grow oats for flavor knowing full well that a plate of oats is richer and more robust when it's grown for taste. The flavor of our oats has also caught the eye of "superstar" chef Dan Barber who loves the taste of our rolled oats so much that he uses our oat groats in his Blue Hill Restaurant in New York. Oat groats hold up better than rice under heat or chafing plates, and they don't break down or become sticky like rice; this has turned many chefs, like Dan, into fans. And as you'll see in the recipes at the back of the book: Amazing local chefs, like Ryan Nitschke of Luna Fargo/Sol Ave. Kitchen and Andrea Baumgardner of BernBaum's, are fans as well.

Oat groats — or, as I call them, oat berries — are the whole grain pieces before they're rolled or steel cut. In addition to having the most exceptional flavor, they're also the most nutritional, and cook much like wild rice. Several James Beard award-winning chefs, including Chef Barber, have used Minnesota oats from our farm in place of rice for risottos and even sushi. Flavorful meals with a local, Midwest twist. Of course, we always knew that oats were great for breakfast. They can be eaten plain, or served as "overnight oats" by putting ¼ cup of rolled oats into a cup of yogurt, or even dressed up with a variety of nuts and fruits to provide an ideal Midwest Mediterranean breakfast. (Some personal favorite toppings for breakfast oats include honey, dried apples, or chopped walnuts with aronia berries. Blueberries and currants are also amazing. If you really want a treat, cook rolled oats in apple juice instead of water and add a dash of cinnamon.)

In general, oats are a simple food that can stand alone, but they can also be added to almost any meal. This can range from mixing oats into a meatloaf to make the meat go further, to crafting your own quick energy bites, or even following the lead of our Seventh Day Adventist friends with plant-based meatballs.

For the Midwest Mediterranean cuisine, local oats are the *ideal* whole grain. They can be used in a wide variety of recipes and dishes that complement and enhance the well-known benefits of the Mediterranean diet. They taste great, they're great for you — and perhaps, one of the most important reasons why organic, whole oats belong in the Midwest Mediterranean diet—they're also great for the land and for the future generations that will follow us.

CHAPTER FOUR
YOUR MENTAL HEALTH
& THE MEDITERRANEAN DIET

WILLIAM SCHULTZ, MA, MHP

Over the past two decades, the most well-studied and widely used interventions for the treatment of depression have been psychotropic drugs and psychotherapy. Recently however, researchers have shown increasing interest in exploring alternative approaches which move beyond therapy and medication. One of the approaches now coming into its own is *nutrition*. Broadly referred to as *nutritional psychiatry*, this area of research is rapidly expanding, largely due to a collection of powerful and promising controlled studies that examine the impact of Mediterranean-style eating on depressive symptoms. This chapter briefly reviews recent research that studies the connection between reduction in depressive symptoms and the Mediterranean diet.

The most prominent trial investigating the effects of a Mediterranean diet on depression is the SMILES study — Supporting the Modification of Lifestyle Interventions in Lowered Emotional States. The SMILES study was a randomized controlled trial consisting of 67 individuals diagnosed with major depressive disorder. Those receiving the dietary intervention were provided in-depth dietary recommendations rooted in the ModiMedDiet, an established form of the Mediterranean diet, and basic social support. The control group for the study was provided basic social support with no dietary change. Both groups saw significant improvement in depressive symptoms — but the dietary intervention group *doubled* their reduction in depressive symptoms compared to the control group. The comparative advantage of the Mediterranean diet group relative to the control group was striking.

Even more surprising was the magnitude of the effect a Mediterranean diet had in reducing depressive symptoms. To appreciate the power of the Mediterranean diet in this way, we need to better understand some of the components of the SMILES study. The SMILES study used a depression measurement tool called the Montgomery-Åsberg Depression Rating Scale (MADRS). Because it allows researchers to track the impact of a specific intervention approach, this kind of measurement tool is the standard and best practice in studies examining an intervention's effect on depressive symptoms. The MADRS has been used in studies measuring the impact of numerous interventions on depressive symptoms, including: psychotherapy, psychotropic drugs, and exercise. The SMILES study used the MADRS to identify a baseline severity of depression score in its participants. The higher the MADRS score, the more severe the depression. In the SMILES study, the average baseline MADRS score of the Mediterranean diet group was approximately 25. After the SMILES study was complete, the average MADRS score of the Mediterranean diet group had been lowered to approximately 15. Thus, individuals participating in the Mediterranean diet saw a noticeable decrease in their depressive symptoms by around 10 MADRS points.

How does the reduction in depression documented in the SMILES study compare to other interventions designed to reduce depressive symptoms?

To put the true power of the Mediterranean diet into perspective, consider that a typical reduction in MADRS scores for individuals participating in trials of psychotropic drugs, such as Prozac, is somewhere between 10 and 15. A typical reduction in MADRS scores for individuals participating in trials of psychotherapy, such as cognitive behavioral therapy, is also between 10 and 15. In other words, the SMILES trial found that a Mediterranean diet had around the same potency in reducing MADRS scores as psychotropic drugs and psychotherapy interventions.

(To be fair, studying the effects of nutrition on depression severity is challenging because of the numerous factors involved as well as the difficulty in effectively "blinding" participants in controlled studies. In randomized controlled trials, participants need to be blinded for the purpose of parsing out the intervention effect from the placebo effect. Blinding is important because we know that *all* interventions for depression have a powerful placebo effect. For example, participants in drug studies are randomized between receiving an active drug or a placebo and participants aren't meant to know if they're getting the active drug or the placebo (that is, they are "blind" to which pill they are taking). This blinding is generally not viable in nutritional studies because it's hard to blind individuals to what food they're eating. On the other hand, it should be noted that most drug trials fail, despite their best intentions, to effectively blind their participants and there are numerous lingering concerns about blinding in psychotherapy trials!)

The sheer magnitude of the effect in the SMILES study was so large that the study was subject to heavy scrutiny. It's fair to say — in fact, the authors of the SMILES study explicitly pointed out — that the takeaway value of the SMILES study will benefit from robust replication. There are also methodological kinks to iron out. Still, a promising replication of the SMILES study has already occurred and, in 2021, a premier team of researchers conducted a sweeping review of the effects of nutrition on mental health and concluded, among many other important findings, that "...relatively convincing data from RCTs (randomized controlled trials) and prospective cohort studies suggest the Mediterranean diet and other healthy dietary patterns may assist in the prevention of depressive illnesses and potentially in the management of depression. These dietary patterns emphasize seafood, olive oil, vegetables, fruits, nuts, lean protein sources, whole grains, and vegetable oils, and limit nutrient-poor, energy-dense foods high in added sugars and saturated fats, including sugar-sweetened beverages, pastries, and refined grains."

In sum, all competent mental health researchers know that depression and other mental disorders are complex phenomena and we ought to be wary of magical cures. However, if the promising initial data from the SMILES study continues to be replicated, then it may well be that one of our most potent interventions for reducing depression is the adoption of a Mediterranean diet.

CHAPTER FIVE
THE MEDITERRANEAN DIET
IS GOOD FOR YOUR HEART

🌿 DAVID CLARDY, MD

Heart disease is the number one cause of death in the U.S. — and much of the western world. Approximately 18 million people are lost worldwide each year due to heart disease. In the U.S., 650,000 people die of heart disease every year; 1 person dies from heart disease every 36 seconds.

As a cardiologist in the upper Midwest for nearly 30 years, I know these sobering statistics are also true for our home. I have seen patients of all ages, races, and walks of life suffering from the ill effects of this terrible disease — a disease we now know is largely preventable by lifestyle. In recent decades, the major cardiology organizations — such as the American College of Cardiology, the American Heart Association, and the American Congress of Preventive Cardiology — have all come to recognize and emphasize the importance of "lifestyle" in the management of heart health. This, of course, includes regular exercise, a healthy diet, proper sleep, good stress management, seasonal influenza vaccinations, and strong social connections, among many other practices. In my experience working as a clinician, I believe many Midwesterners do several things quite well with regards to lifestyle. I see many people who get proper sleep, have strong social connections, and who regularly visit their doctor for vaccines and check-ups. However, an area that I have noted many in the upper Midwest can improve upon is that of diet. Today's Standard American Diet (or SAD diet, as a clever acronym) has left many struggling with chronic health issues, including my specialty: coronary artery disease (CAD). However, this diagnosis is not written in stone and with slight dietary modifications, many can find themselves in a vastly improved state of health, while eating a more balanced, healthful — and possibly even more delicious! – diet. Therefore, within the context of this book, the major component of a heart-healthy lifestyle that I'd like to discuss is diet. There are several diets that have been shown to reduce morbidity and mortality caused by heart disease. By far, one of the most popular of such diets – one which has shown enormous benefits – is the Mediterranean diet.

Foods for the Heart

As we've already learned in Chapters One and Two, the Mediterranean diet is based on the cuisines consumed by people living in the countries around the Mediterranean Sea, which research studies have shown is associated with reduced cardiovascular disease. Scientific interest in this kind of diet began in the 1960s after it was observed that deaths from coronary artery disease were less frequent in these particular countries when compared to other European countries and the U.S.

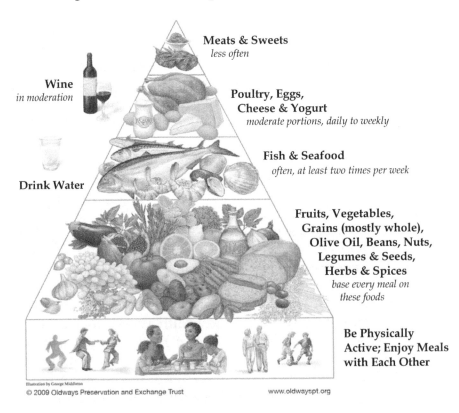

Meats & Sweets
less often

Wine
in moderation

Poultry, Eggs, Cheese & Yogurt
moderate portions, daily to weekly

Fish & Seafood
often, at least two times per week

Drink Water

Fruits, Vegetables, Grains (mostly whole), Olive Oil, Beans, Nuts, Legumes & Seeds, Herbs & Spices
base every meal on these foods

Be Physically Active; Enjoy Meals with Each Other

Illustration by George Middleton

© 2009 Oldways Preservation and Exchange Trust   www.oldwayspt.org

34

The Mediterranean diet, in general, consists of certain characteristic components, as discussed by Megan in Chapter Two. It's typically illustrated as a "food pyramid," with the food types at the bottom being consumed *more* frequently and the food types at the top being consumed *less* frequently. At the base of the pyramid are the carbohydrates. These must be whole grain, non-refined carbohydrates to be beneficial. Also occupying the lower tiers of the pyramid are fruits and vegetables. Like the whole grains described above, these should be consumed in multiple, daily servings. The general health benefits of fruits and vegetables are well known, as they are low in calories and high in antioxidants. With regards to heart health, these foods improve circulation and provide cardiac protection. In addition, fruits and vegetables can also be an excellent source of fiber. The benefits of fiber in the diet, with respect to cardiovascular risk, include the following:

◆ **Lower LDL cholesterol**
◆ **Reduced body inflammation**
◆ **Reduced lipid peroxidation**
◆ **Improved insulin sensitivity**
◆ **Weight reduction**
◆ **Beneficial effect on gut flora**

High serum LDL, or high-density lipoprotein, is a component of the total body cholesterol, often referred to as the "bad" cholesterol. These particles circulate in the blood and are associated with increased risk of coronary disease. Peroxidation is the process by which the LDL becomes oxidized. When that happens, the oxidized LDL becomes atherogenic — meaning that they promote plaque buildup in the arteries. Inflammation then causes these plaques to become unstable, leading them to rupture. Plaque rupture is a primary cause of heart attacks, strokes, and sudden death. As one of the key components of the Mediterranean diet, fiber helps reduce these events.

Also low on the pyramid are nuts, which are high in mono- and polyunsaturated fats. These foods also lower LDL cholesterol levels. Benefit occurs when these fats are consumed in place of saturated fat. In fact, studies have shown regular consumption of nuts more than four times a week substantially lowers the risk of cardiovascular events.

Olive oil plays, perhaps, the most prominent role in the Mediterranean diet. There are many documented heart-healthy benefits of olive oil:

- **Improved lipid profile**
- **Lower postprandial (post-meal) glucose**
- **Anti-inflammatory**
- **Antioxidant**
- **Reduced clot formation in the bloodstream**
- **Improved blood pressure**
- **Reduced risk of heart attack and stroke**

Definite benefits occur when butter is replaced with olive oil. One important caveat: the olive oil *must* be extra-virgin and cold-pressed. Refined olive oil, or olive oil extracted with heat, cannot render the same benefits for a healthy heart.

The vinegar in oil-and-vinegar dressings popular in the Mediterranean diet also has beneficial effects for heart health. Vinegar delays gastric emptying, delays carbohydrate absorption, and reduces postprandial glucose. This results in prolonged satiety, in other words — less hunger — leading to a tendency to eat less.

Fish and shrimp also play a prominent role in the Mediterranean diet. The benefit of these foods for cardiovascular health arises from the high concentration of omega-3 fatty acids in these foods. (Shrimp is also packed with nutrients, protein, and healthy fat; it also has the antioxidant astaxanthin which has been linked in clinical studies to cardiovascular fitness.) Omega 3s are polyunsaturated fats of which there are 3 types: alpha-linolenic acid (ALA), eicosapentaenoic acid (EPA), and docosahexaenoic acid (DHA). EPA and DHA are found in animal and dairy products, with higher amounts in products from grass-fed animals. ALA is found in plant sources, primarily. (Other sources of omega 3s include oysters, flax seeds, chia seeds, and walnuts.) Regular consumption of foods containing omega 3s have been shown to have cardiovascular benefits, some of which are:

- **Improved blood pressure**
- **Lower serum triglycerides**
- **Increased HDL, "good" cholesterol**
- **Lower LDL, "bad" cholesterol**
- **Reduced clot formation in the bloodstream**
- **Reduced plaque buildup in arteries, i.e. less hardening of the arteries**
- **Anti-inflammatory effects**
- **Improved overall heart muscle function**

Yogurt and cheese are other components of the Mediterranean diet that can provide healthy heart benefits, but should be eaten in moderation—about 2 servings daily. Yogurt is an excellent source of protein, calcium, and B vitamins. The yogurt made from cow's milk may have a favorable effect on gut bacteria, as we'll learn in the next chapter, but you can also enjoy yogurt made from almond, soy, or coconut milk. Cheese is also a source of protein, calcium, and B vitamins. Heart healthy cheeses connected to the Mediterranean diet include cottage cheese, feta, mozzarella, parmesan, and provolone, to name a few. These cheeses contain conjugated linoleic acid (CLA), an essential fat primarily found in meat and dairy from grass-fed cows, sheep, and goats. CLA may help to reduce body fat, to build lean muscle, to regulate blood sugar, reduce inflammation, and—once again—to lower the risk of heart disease.

Sweets containing refined sugar and carbohydrates are carefully restricted in the Mediterranean diet. Processed foods with added sugar can have serious adverse effects on cardiovascular fitness. They can cause weight gain, chronic inflammation, insulin resistance leading to diabetes, and poor heart health. All that said, it is still possible to have very nice, healthy desserts and still take care of your heart. Perfect Midwest Mediterranean desserts include fruit that has natural sweetness, yogurt, nuts, extra-virgin olive oil, and whole grains.

Red wine is also an important part of the Mediterranean diet. While the subject of wine in any diet is somewhat controversial with regard to the prescription of alcohol, the documented heart-healthy benefits attributed to red wine are as follows:

- **Raises HDL, "good" cholesterol**
- **Anti-inflammatory effects**
- **Antioxidants (flavonoids, polyphenols, resveratrol)**
- **Reduced clot formation in the bloodstream**
- **Reduced postprandial glucose**
- **Generally lowers cardiovascular risk**

The antioxidants and flavonoids in red wine which appear to bestow heart benefit are found in the skin of the grapes which, of course, gives red wine its color. It's unclear whether white wine, which is aged and fermented without the skin, confers the same benefits as red wine. There are some studies, however, which suggest that alcohol itself provides the primary health benefits. Regardless, it should be remembered that wine should be consumed with meals in order to enjoy the full health benefits. Also, as with any alcoholic beverage, moderation is crucial. 2 drinks or less a day for men and 1 drink or less a day for women. A standard drink of red wine is 5 ounces, or a little more than a ½ cup.

Occupying the very top of the Mediterranean diet pyramid is red meat. It should be consumed only rarely. There are two sources of iron in the Mediterranean diet: red meat and plants. Red meat has *heme iron*, which is the iron found in the blood and muscle of animals. Plants have *non-heme iron*, found in foods like legumes, nuts, and leafy greens. The problem with heme iron is that it is a pro-oxidant, which means that it oxidizes LDL cholesterol. Oxidized LDL in the arteries leads to atherosclerotic plaque formation. High rates of red meat consumption are thus associated with higher risk of coronary artery disease, stroke, and type 2 diabetes. Red meat is also high in saturated fat, which also raises LDL cholesterol. These risks are not associated with non-heme iron found in plants. Iron is important in the diet. However, sufficient amounts of dietary iron can be obtained from plants, without the risks associated with heme iron from red meat. Finally, red meat contains carnitine and choline, which are converted by gut bacteria into trimethylamine which, in turn, is then oxidized by the liver to trimethylamine N-oxide or TMAO. TMAO then enters the bloodstream and can promote the development of atherosclerosis. Plants common in the Mediterranean diet have compounds which neutralize the production of TMAO. Based on the considerations above, consumption of red meat should be limited, ideally to no more than twice a month. Processed meats—such as sausage, baloney, salami, and hot dogs—all promote atherosclerosis, weight gain, cancer, and hypertension; they have no place in the Mediterranean diet.

All of this is fairly well known to the medical community. That said, in the last couple decades, there has been a renewed interest in the Mediterranean diet. Extensive research, observational studies, and a myriad of scientific papers have been published, all tending to support the premise that this diet is overall a healthy diet, particularly with regard to cardiovascular fitness. In this context, I'd like to mention two studies out of the multitude which make this point.

Case Studies to Consider
The first is the PREDIMED study out of Spain which randomized 7,447 high-risk persons and placed them on either a low-fat diet or the Mediterranean diet. This was a "primary prevention study," which means the subjects enrolled in the study did *not* have any clinical or known heart disease. Incredibly, the study was stopped prematurely for ethical reasons after less than five years. Why? Because of the extraordinary reduction in heart attacks and strokes for the test subjects that were placed on the Mediterranean diet. With those unequivocal results, continuing the trial and keeping the other subjects on the inferior, low-fat diet would have been immoral. The Mediterranean diet is that impactful.

Another recent study was the Lyon Diet Heart Study. In contrast to the Spanish study mentioned above, this was a "secondary study," which means that the subjects already had clinical heart disease; they had *already* suffered heart attacks. This study explored the likelihood of further progression of heart disease among subjects on various diets. When the Mediterranean diet was compared to the typical western diet, once again, the results were amazing. The conclusions are illustrated here:

Lyon Diet Heart Study
605 patients following a myocardial infarction randomized to a Mediterranean* or Western** diet for 4 years

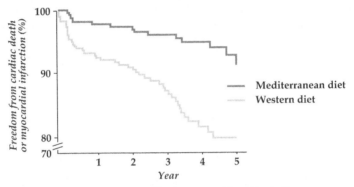

*High in polyunsaturated fat and fiber; **High in saturated fat and low in fiber

As you can see, the incidence of a recurrent myocardial infarction (heart attack) or cardiac death was significantly reduced on the Mediterranean diet. These studies represent two examples of the scientific evidence supporting the cardiac benefits of the Mediterranean diet.

In sum, the interconnected, mutually reinforcing heart benefits of the Mediterranean diet are as follows:

♦ **Improved blood pressure**
♦ **Lower serum triglycerides**
♦ **Increased HDL, "good" cholesterol**
♦ **Reduced LDL, "bad" cholesterol**
♦ **Improved endothelial function and circulation**
♦ **Reduced clot formation in the bloodstream**

- Reduced postprandial glucose
- Antioxidants
- Reduced plaque buildup in arteries, resulting in the slowing of artery hardening
- Anti-inflammatory effects
- Weight reduction
- Improved lipid profile
- Improved overall heart muscle function

Perhaps most importantly, based on the weight of scientific and clinical evidence, the more rigorously a person adheres to the Mediterranean diet, the healthier that person's heart and cardiovascular system will be.

In conclusion, the Mediterranean diet represents a major component of a healthy lifestyle, specifically with regards to heart health. As you read in the previous chapters, our region grows many of the foods that are cornerstones of the Mediterranean diet, and with the amazing, globalized food system we enjoy today—we can beautifully blend the foods of our region with the flavors, key ingredients, and cooking techniques of Mediterranean cuisine to create a perfectly local, and unique, Midwest Mediterranean diet! And as you'll see in the recipes at the end of this book, this heart healthy diet is very flexible and can be achieved in many ways. Perhaps just as important: The Mediterranean diet is made up of foods that are very delicious!

Bon appétit!

CHAPTER SIX
YOUR GUT & THE MEDITERRANEAN DIET

FADEL NAMMOUR, MD

The Mediterranean Sea is often considered the cradle of civilization and its people's dietary model is one of the healthiest in the world: a simple, nonrestrictive diet that relies on adequate daily water intake, regular social and physical activity, and a handful of essential, unprocessed ingredients. Thus, the benefits of the Mediterranean diet are due not to a single, isolated factor, but rather to a synergic and interactive combination of nutrients, environments, and lifestyle choices. In recent years, the human microbiota—the web of microorganisms within each human body—has emerged as a critical element in and for human health. Unsurprisingly, in numerous studies, the Mediterranean diet has been shown to play a major role in maintaining a healthy intestinal microbiota, especially when compared to other diets. As this is my specific area of expertise, in this chapter, we'll explore the interaction between microbiota, the Mediterranean diet, and human wellness.

Let's start with our microbiota.

All humans have different communities of microorganisms in our noses, our mouths, our respiratory systems, and our skin—but the bulk of our microbes are in our gut. Unlike our genes, which are relatively constant, our microbiome changes from birth to adulthood and can be affected dramatically by our choices, environments, and diets. Our microbiota also can be altered by medications, especially antibiotics, and by disease. Of course, modern science has traditionally viewed the human body as a set of distinct, interdependent organs that connect and work under the control of the brain. For this reason, standard models of medicine and surgery focus on providing tools and procedures designed to fix each organ when it no longer functions.

Recently—as technologies and lifestyles have changed and as traditional scientific methodologies have revealed their limits—these models have been challenged. It has become clear that our bodies and organs are best understood not as a set of distinct operating parts but rather as complex, fully integrated wholes. Particularly important for us here, we now know that our bodies rely on a "brain-gut axis" regulated by complex mechanisms that are dominated by our microbiota.

The brain-gut axis is defined as a bidirectional link between the central nervous system, the brain, and the enteric nervous system, also referred to as our "second brain." The enteric nervous system is embedded in the walls of the digestive system. Although it functions quite differently from the brain in our head, our second brain communicates with our "first brain" constantly. This relationship has profound results on our health, well-being, and behavior. Have you ever made a decision based on a "gut feeling?" Or felt "butterflies in your stomach?" Or had a "gut-wrenching" experience that left your stomach tied up in knots? These common phrases have concrete, scientific explanations.

The connection between the cognitive and emotional centers in the brain and peripheral intestinal function involves our neurons, hormones, and immune systems. Microbiota can communicate with human cells via neuronal signals (neurotransmitters), endocrine signals (hormones and regulatory gut peptides), or immune signals (cytokines). Numerous studies have demonstrated that the microbes in our body play a major role in regulating this complex process, resulting in a healthy and balanced internal "environment" for our microbiota. Thanks to very recent advances in genome sequencing, scientists have been able to identify the various different species of organisms that comprise our microbiota as well as better understand their functions and their interactions with their hosts—us. We now know that the body contains trillions of microorganisms, outnumbering human cells 10 to 1. The rest of our bodies consist of our microbiome. In this sense, these microbe communities truly define who and what we are. Most of the time, the interaction between microbes and humans is a symbiotic relationship, either defined as *mutualism*—when both partners benefit—or as *commensalism*—when one partner benefits and the other is unharmed. The key takeaway here is that our microbes' primary goal is to survive and multiply — that means they want to keep *us* healthy.

How is all of this connected to the Mediterranean diet?

Our microbiomes can be altered by what we eat. A flood of new research demonstrates that a Mediterranean diet can have a positive impact on our microbiome. Various recent studies have tracked the differences between microbiome composition in obese vs. lean donors, diabetics vs. non-diabetics, and even children on the autism spectrum vs. unaffected siblings. In all instances, the Mediterranean diet emerges as one of the healthiest dietary patterns. In other clinical studies, adherence to a Mediterranean diet follows a "scoring system" based on the consumption of Mediterranean-style vegetables, legumes, cereals, fish, meat, dairy products, alcohol, and—especially—extra-virgin olive oil. The higher the score, the healthier the diet. Once again, in these studies, the Mediterranean diet has been associated with decreased mortality and decreased chronic diseases ranging from cardiovascular disease to stroke, to diabetes, to liver disease— even to allergies. The Mediterranean diet also has been shown to reduce the incidence of cancer and to prevent cognitive decline— other areas of study now being connected to healthy microbiota.

One prominent theory as to the effect of the Mediterranean diet on holistic human health lies in the way in which the Mediterranean diet affects microbiota behavior, development, and composition. Eating food—and the subsequent microbial fermentation taking place in the gut—always leads to chemical byproducts which can directly or indirectly affect human metabolism, immune response, and general well-being. If these microbial processes are positive, then they will have a positive impact on your overall health; if they are negative, then they will not. A healthy gut contains at least a thousand different species of organisms, including two important phyla: the *Firmicutes* and the *Bacteroidetes*. The ratio of these two phyla — the Firmicutes/Bacteroidetes ratio, or F/B ratio — has emerged as a promising biomarker for general and specific health conditions. (For example, the F/B ratio is frequently cited in scientific literature as a marker for obesity, inflammatory bowel disease, and type 2 diabetes; the higher ratio — that is to say, the more Firmicutes you have — the higher the incidence of these issues.) A healthy gut also contains a wide variety of fungi, archaea, and viruses; this internal diversity is also extremely important. As you might have already guessed, studies have shown that individuals who consumed a diet with a higher Mediterranean diet score had a more diverse microbiome with a lower F/B ratio. A lower F/B ratio has been shown to:

♦ **Support the immune system**
♦ **Reduce inflammation**
♦ **Aid liver metabolism and detoxification pathways**
♦ **Reduce insulin resistance**
♦ **Protect against other pathogens**
♦ **Prevent and correct fatigue disorders**
♦ **Eliminate brain fog and aid mental clarity**
♦ **Improve general stamina and physical performance**

Conversely, individuals with a *lower* adherence to a Mediterranean diet demonstrated an increase in the bacteria *streptococcaceae*, especially the genus *streptococcus*, which is associated with higher body mass index and increased inflammatory status. Streptococcus has been associated with multiple diseases in humans including gingivitis, strep throat, impetigo, cellulitis, and kidney disease to name a few. Further studies have shown the benefits of supplementing our diets with good bacteria (probiotic) and good fiber (prebiotic) for the treatment or prevention of certain diseases, many of which occur naturally in the Mediterranean diet. It is important to keep in mind that these research and findings are still in their early stages. Even so, the results are promising and consistently point to the value of the Mediterranean diet for a healthy gut.

One key ingredient of the Mediterranean diet specifically connected to wellness is *extra-virgin olive oil*. As we've just learned from David, extra-virgin olive oil and its polyphenol compounds have been associated with several documented health benefits such as preventing metabolic syndrome, reducing hypertension, and decreasing incidents of cardiovascular disease, chronic inflammation, and cancer. Extra-virgin olive oil not only decreases lipid and protein oxidation, it actually increases glutathione enzyme levels. These important enzymes can play huge roles as incredible free radical scavengers; several observational studies in humans have shown that they can modify our gut microbiota in a very positive way.

Studies comparing diets enriched with olive oil to diets enriched with butter have shown the following beneficial microbial changes:

- Increase in *bifidobacterial,* which have antioxidant activities.
- Decrease in *Desulfovibrionaceae* and *alistipes indistinctus*, which correlates with improved insulin levels and blood pressure.
- Increase in *Sutterellaceae, Marispirillum,* and *Mucilaginibacter dageonensis,* which correlates with reduced leptin levels, the hormone that helps regulate hunger.
- Increase in *Clostridia XIVa,* a butyrate producing bacteria, which may be useful against chronic inflammation and lowering blood pressure.
- Increase in *bacteroidaceae* family (*B. fragilis* species), which lead to lower Firmicutes to Bacteroides ratio and all its attendant benefits.

It's critical to note these benefits have been documented more so with cold-pressed, extra-virgin olive oil than "regular" olive oil.

Perhaps one of the most important aspects of the Mediterranean diet is the consistent presence of foods that have been subjected to *fermentation*. Fermentation is a natural anaerobic process in which microorganisms like bacteria, yeast, and fungi convert food into simpler compounds that produce short fatty acid chains and energy. Humans learned to control this process centuries ago for a variety of purposes. Celebrating with an alcoholic beverage and eating a healthier, more bioavailable bread due to the fermentation process are just a couple of the many well-known examples.

Fermented foods have been used for centuries around the Mediterranean basin to treat illnesses. In the 16th century, for example, the Ottoman Sultan Suleiman the Magnificent sent his personal physician to treat Francis I of France who was suffering from diarrhea. The Turkish physician treated and cured the king with yogurt made of sheep's milk, thus introducing yogurt to the West.

Other common fermented foods sometimes associated with aspects of the Mediterranean diet include:

- **Kefir: originated, perhaps, in Russia, although some scholars attribute the word to the Turkish language meaning "foam "or "long life" or "good life." Shepherds discovered that fresh milk carried in leather pouches would ferment into an effervescent beverage. Today, Kefir is prepared by adding a specific combination of bacteria and yeast (kefir grains) to cow, goat, or sheep milk.**
- **Raw cheese: made with milk that has not been pasteurized and has been aged 6 months or more.**
- **Kombucha: black tea leaves and sugar mixed with bacteria and yeast.**
- **Sauerkraut: one of the oldest traditional foods, made from fermented green or red cabbage.**
- **Pickles: in the Mediterranean and Middle East, fermented pickles are made with brine (salt and water), not vinegar.**

- Miso: a traditional Japanese ingredient made by fermenting soybean, barley, or brown rice with fungus *Koji*. (Clearly not Mediterranean, but worth noting all the same!)
- Tempeh: made of soybeans with a mix of live mold.

As you read in Megan and Noreen's chapters, the upper Midwest is home to amazing, diverse food production, but our ill-tempered northern climate has necessitated the use of many food preservation techniques—including fermentation. When German immigrants came to the north in the late 19th century, they brought their fermentation knowledge to turn cabbage into sauerkraut and barley into beer, and Scandinavian immigrants, a dairy-centric culture, brought a wide assortment of techniques to turn milk into a variety of fermented dairy products, like yogurt and soured milks.

Natural fermentation occurring in the human body can positively affect our well-being and our health. Recent studies have shown that the microbes living within our body are able to communicate, regulate, and sustain our organs in harmonious balance through fermentation processes. And how is this fermentation process initiated within our bodies? By eating for your microbiota!

Clearly, the "food is your medicine movement" has gained wider acceptance over the last two decades. With ever-rising health care costs and our natural yearning to live longer and healthier lives, we are turning to healthier diets that are increasingly backed by scientific data. More and more practitioners and clinicians see food as a part of viable therapeutic options. Sometime around 400 B.C.E., the Greek physician Hippocrates supposedly said, "Let food be thy Medicine and Medicine be thy food." When it comes to the health of our guts, this maxim is perfectly captured by the Mediterranean diet.

Conclusion
Final Thoughts at the Table . . .

As we conclude Midwest Mediterranean, we hope you'll share our opinion that this diet — or lifestyle, as we should really call it — is truly something exceptional. By bringing together the healthy, sustainably grown foods of the upper Midwest, in combination with the key ingredients, flavors, and techniques of the Mediterranean, along with the knowledge of this diet's history, an appreciation for the food of our region, and medical knowledge — this little book is truly something unique and special.

However, reading can only get you so far.

In order to understand how truly awesome this idea is, you really must taste it.

That's why we conclude this book with a collection of amazing recipes from chefs and home cooks from across the Midwest and the Mediterranean. The folks who shared these recipes are truly the best of the best. Not only do they cook it, but they live it! You will see ingredients and techniques that are familiar, and others that may be new. You'll see recommendations to source an ingredient from a specific Midwest farmer, like oat groats from Noreen Thomas, or the use of a high-quality Mediterranean ingredient, like extra-virgin olive oil from Mistras Estates. These recommendations are key! In the famous words of Alice Waters, "When you have the best and tastiest ingredients, you can cook very simply, and the food will be extraordinary, because it tastes like what it is."

We are blessed to have some of the best and tastiest ingredients right in our backyard, and some brought to us from our friends across the world, to create extraordinary Midwest Mediterranean food.

Finally, as we developed this little book of Midwest Mediterranean principles and particulars, the most thrilling part was the idea of the "eclectic community table" that we hope you will create. As you develop your own delicious table using these foods and ideas, we hope you will share it so others and let them discover this truly amazing way of eating and living.

Bon Appétit!

 ## Appendix A

Mediterranean Recipes for the High Plains

1. **Triple Olive Dip** | Sarah Nasello

2. **Summer Chickpea Salad** | Megan Lewis

3. **Squash and Apple Tabbouleh** | Chef Andrea Baumgardner

4. **Oat Groats and Crispy Kale with Wild Mushrooms and Caper Butter** | Chef Ryan Nitschke

5. **The Ultimate Greek Salad** | Peter Schultz, PhD

6. **Midwest Mediterranean Bean Salad** | Megan Myrdal, MS; RD

7. **Briam (Greek Roasted Vegetables)** | Eugene Ladopoulos

8. **Roasted! Fall and Winter Midwest Vegetables** | Duane and Karen Ehrens, RD

9. **Ιμάμ-Μπαϊλντί - Imám Bayildí ("Fainting Imam," Stuffed Eggplant)** | Giannis Ladopoulos

10. **Patatas Bravas (Spicy Potatoes)** | Sam Wai

11. **Dairy-Free Italian Stuffed Bell Peppers** | Kayla Coté van Rensburg

12. **Corfu Rooster with Bucatini Pasta** | Gary Litt

13. **Mediterranean Spaghetti with Lobster** | David Clardy, MD

14. **Gastrin, A Traditional Minoan Dessert** | Georgios Maltezakis

15. **Blackboard Olive Oil Lemon Bundt Cake with Lemon Curd and Lavender Cream Cheese Icing** | Terri Trickle

TRIPLE OLIVE DIP

Sarah Nasello
Chef, Restauranteur, Food Writer

YIELD ~ Serves many!
PREP TIME ~ 15 minutes
COOKING TIME ~ 15 minutes (Plus at least 30 minutes to allow flavors to meld.)

INGREDIENTS

- ½ cup (4 ounces) good extra-virgin olive oil, plus extra for garnish
- 2 cloves garlic, minced
- 1 tsp balsamic vinegar
- 1 cup tomatoes, diced small
- Kosher salt, to taste
- ½ cup kalamata olives, pitted, roughly chopped
- ½ cup green olives, pitted, roughly chopped
- 4 ounces feta cheese, crumbled
- 1 tbsp fresh basil, thinly sliced (chiffonade style)
- Freshly ground black pepper

DIRECTIONS

1. Pour the oil in the bottom of a shallow bowl or platter. Stir in the garlic until combined. Drizzle the balsamic vinegar over the oil mixture.

2. Place the diced tomatoes in a wide mound in the center of the dish and add a sprinkling of kosher salt. Add the olives and feta cheese and drizzle with extra-virgin olive oil. Garnish with the basil strips and freshly ground black pepper.

3. Serve with good, crusty bread. This dipping oil is best when prepared at least 30 minutes before serving so that the flavors can meld together.

Summer Chickpea Salad

Megan Lewis
Cheesemonger, Milk Made Catering

We love this fresh and delicious side for summertime grilling. Filled with fresh vegetables, chickpeas, and herbs, it is refreshing and tasty!

YIELD ~ Serves 6
PREP TIME ~ 25 minutes
TOTAL TIME ~ 25 minutes

INGREDIENTS

- 15-ounce can of chickpeas
- 2 medium garlic cloves, minced
- 1 small red onion, chopped
- 1 sweet yellow bell pepper, chopped
- 2 cups cherry tomatoes, halved
- 1 English cucumber, seeded and diced
- ½ cup feta cheese, crumbled
- 1 tbsp extra-virgin olive oil
- 3 tbsp fresh lemon juice
- 2 tbsp fresh herbs (dill, chives, parsley, etc.)
- Salt and pepper, to taste

DIRECTIONS

1. In a medium bowl, add prepared chickpeas, red onion, bell pepper, tomatoes, cucumber, and feta cheese. Toss to combine.
2. In a small bowl, whisk together olive oil and lemon juice. Add garlic and fresh herbs. Season to taste with salt and pepper.
3. Pour over chickpea salad and stir well. Enjoy!

SQUASH AND APPLE TABBOULEH

Chef Andrea Baumgardner
Co-Owner, BernBaum's

Tabbouleh is a refreshing herb and bulgur salad from the Middle East. Although it is traditionally made with copious amounts of parsley and mint, a bit of tomato, cucumber, bulgur, and lemon, we adapted it to local ingredients at BernBaum's. We serve it mixed with greens as a salad or with beet hummus and baba ghanoush. Don't be afraid to change it up — whatever is in season will work.

YIELD ~ 6 servings (1-cup portions)
PREP TIME ~ 30 minutes
TOTAL TIME ~ 45 minutes

INGREDIENTS

- 1 cup oat groats (we buy ours from Doubting Thomas Farms), soaked overnight in 2 cups water (optional)
- 1 tsp kosher salt
- 3 cups water
- 2 - 2 ½ cups winter squash, peeled and medium diced (1 butternut squash or 2 acorn)
- 1 tbsp extra-virgin olive oil (we use Mistra Estates)
- ½ tsp kosher salt (we prefer Diamond Crystal — less salty)
- 1 apple, medium-sized, diced small
- ½ cup each of fresh herbs, a mixture of parsley, dill, fennel tops, and scallion
- 2 tbsp lemon juice
- 1-2 tsp kosher salt

DIRECTIONS

1. If the oat groats were soaked overnight, drain them and place in a saucepan with 1 tsp of kosher salt and 3 cups of water. Bring to a simmer and cook until tender, 15-20 minutes.

Remove from heat, drain water, and pour groats onto a sheet pan to cool. Set aside.

2. Toss winter squash with olive oil and a sprinkle of salt. Spread onto a baking sheet and roast at 400° F until the edges of the squash are browning and it is cooked throughout, but not mushy. Set aside to cool.

3. When cool, mix together oat groats, apple, squash, fresh herbs, lemon, and salt. Season to taste. Store in the refrigerator for up to 3 days. Serve mixed with greens or as an al fresco side dish.

OTHER WINNING COMBINATIONS TO REPLACE SQUASH & APPLE

SUMMER

- *grilled summer squash and green beans*
- *the classic: tomato and cucumber*
- *peppers and chickpeas*

WINTER

- *pomegranate and fennel*
- *cucumber and orange*

SPRING

- *snap pea and asparagus*

Oat Groats and Crispy Kale with Wild Mushrooms and Caper Butter

Chef Ryan Nitschke

Co-Owner, Luna Fargo / Sol Ave. Kitchen

We use the spirit of this dish in many incarnations at both of my restaurants. I mostly love the versatility of this dish, as well as its simplicity. It's like a choose your own adventure book, but for dinner. Instead of oat groats you can use almost any other grain you prefer, like farro, freekeh, barley, wild rice, and on and on. Instead of kale, use collard greens or spinach; use any type of mushrooms you can find or substitute any fresh veggies from your garden; use any mix of herbs you can get your hands on for the butter. I think you get the point. The end result will be a fresh and vibrant side dish to pair with a protein or as a standalone entrée for a tasty lunch or dinner.

YIELD ~ 4-6 sides or 2-3 entrées
PREP TIME ~ 35 minutes
TOTAL TIME ~ 60 minutes

INGREDIENTS

- 2 cups oat groats, soaked in water overnight
- 8 ounces kale, cleaned and trimmed
- 8 ounces wild mushrooms, cleaned and sliced
- 4 ounces butter (one stick), room temperature
- 3 tbsp capers, minced
- 3 garlic cloves, minced
- 1 small shallot, minced
- 1 tsp chili flakes
- 2 tbsp mixed herbs, roughly chopped
- Kosher salt and ground black pepper
- Neutral oil for cooking such as rice or grapeseed

DIRECTIONS

1. In a small sauce pot, add soaked oats with 3 cups cooking liquid. You can use water, or, as we like to use, chicken or vegetable broth. Place on burner on medium to high heat and cook until liquid has been fully absorbed by the oats, about 15 minutes. Remove from heat.

2. Meanwhile, preheat oven to 350° F. In a large bowl, toss kale with enough oil just to barely coat, about 2 tbsp. Season lightly with salt and pepper. Toss to combine and lay out on a baking pan. Place in the oven for 10-15 minutes or until kale is just crispy. It should still have its beautiful color. Remove from oven and reserve for finishing.

3. For the caper butter, you can use a food processor, a mixer, or combine by hand in a mixing bowl. Simply combine butter, capers, garlic, shallot, chili flakes, and herbs (we use rosemary, thyme, parsley, and chives). Season with salt and pepper to taste. Set aside and reserve for finishing.

4. To finish, heat a large sauté pan on medium to high heat. Add 2-3 tbsp of oil followed by the mushrooms (I love chanterelles). Cook mushrooms until just tender, about 5 minutes, stirring frequently. Add cooked oat groats and continue to stir and cook until heated through, about 3 minutes. Add as much or as little of the caper butter as you prefer. Save whatever you don't use for later use. Before butter is fully melted in, add the kale. Gently crumble it as you add it in. Stir, mix, and taste. Season with salt and pepper as needed. Remove from heat and serve immediately.

❧ THE ULTIMATE GREEK SALAD

Peter Schultz, PhD
Conservationist, Archaeologist, Importer

In Greece there's an expression that goes like this: "Ηελληνική κουζίνα είναι πολύ κοντά στη φύση." Or: "Greek cuisine is very close to nature." Nowhere is this more true than in the case of the classical Greek salad. In Greece, this salad is called a "χωριάτικη σαλάτα" – literally, a "country salad." Its ingredients consist of chopped vegetables and feta cheese dressed with salt, pepper, and extra-virgin, cold-pressed olive oil. It is an exercise in simplicity.

YIELD ~ One large Greek salad for one hungry person. Multiply this recipe x1 for each additional setting.
PREP TIME ~ 15 minutes
TOTAL TIME ~ 15 minutes

INGREDIENTS

- 1 ½ ripe tomatoes, cut into rough chunks, never cubed or diced
- ½ cucumber, peeled and thickly cross-sliced
- ¼ red onion, cut into strips
- ¼ green pepper, cut into strips
- ½ banana pepper, thickly cross-sliced (optional)
- 2 ounces Greek feta cheese (1 or 2 rough chunks), never crumbled
- 7 pitted kalamata olives
- 1 tsp salt
- 1 tsp pepper
- 1 tsp oregano (optional)
- ¼ cup cold-pressed, extra-virgin olive oil

DIRECTIONS

1. In a large bowl, place your prepared tomatoes, cucumbers, red onions, peppers, feta chunks, and olives. Season to taste with salt, pepper, and oregano (optional). Dress with olive oil. Enjoy!

MIDWEST MEDITERRANEAN BEAN SALAD

Megan Myrdal, MS; RD

Co-Founder, Food of the North

This salad is the perfect combination of ingredients and flavors from the Mediterranean, paired with wonderful foods grown in the Midwest. Legumes (a term that encompasses beans, peas, chickpeas, and lentils) are often overlooked and undervalued in the Midwestern diet, but they are exceptionally nutritious, enjoyed in abundance in the Mediterranean diet, and bonus — they are grown all across the Midwest! This salad can be enjoyed as a side or as a meal on its own!

YIELD ~ 12, 1-cup portions
PREP TIME ~ 30 minutes
TOTAL TIME ~ 30 minutes

INGREDIENTS

For the Salad:

- 3 cups whole wheat couscous, prepared according to package instructions
- 1, 15-ounce can dark red kidney beans, drained and rinsed
- 1, 15-ounce can cannellini beans, drained and rinsed
- 1, 15-ounce can garbanzo beans, drained and rinsed
- 2 cups kale, washed, stemmed, and finely shredded
- 1 cup cucumbers, washed, peeled, and sliced into ½ moons
- 1 cup cherry tomatoes, washed, sliced in half
- ½ cup red onion, thinly sliced
- ¼ cup each of parsley, mint, and basil, washed and roughly chopped
- ½ cup pitted kalamata olives
- 1 cup feta cheese

For the Balsamic Vinaigrette Dressing:

- ⅓ cup balsamic vinegar
- 2 tbsp Dijon mustard
- 2 garlic cloves, minced
- 1 cup Mistra Estates extra-virgin olive oil
- Salt and pepper, to taste

DIRECTIONS

1. Combine all prepared salad ingredients in a large bowl.
2. In a small bowl, combine vinegar, mustard, and garlic. Add the oil in a steady stream, whisking constantly. Season with salt and pepper to taste.
3. Mix dressing into salad and enjoy!

🫒 BRIAM (GREEK ROASTED VEGETABLES)

Eugene Ladopoulos
Owner & Farmer, Mistra Estates

Briam is a traditional Greek recipe of roasted vegetables and extra-virgin olive oil. This dish is Eugene Ladopoulos's version of the classic recipe. Eugene is the owner and maker of Mistra Estates Extra Virgin Olive Oil. Mistra Estates extra-virgin olive oil has a high resistance to heat and helps mix all different vegetable flavors together while adding its own complex aroma.

YIELD ~ 6 or more servings
PREP TIME ~ 20 minutes
TOTAL TIME ~ 1 hour, 20 minutes

INGREDIENTS

- 4-5 medium sized potatoes, thinly sliced across
- 4-5 eggplants, thinly sliced across, preferably of two different varieties (a dark wide variety and a slimmer stripped one, the slimmer one cut in smaller round pieces)
- 4-5 zucchini, thinly sliced across
- 2 red bell peppers, thinly sliced (optional)
- 2 cloves of garlic, sliced (optional)
- Parsley, preferably fresh, coarsely chopped
- 4 large onions, cut in four
- 1, 28-ounce can crushed tomatoes
- Mistra Estates extra-virgin olive oil
- Oregano, dried
- Salt and black pepper

DIRECTIONS

1. Preheat oven to 400° F.
2. Cover bottom of an oven-safe baking dish with extra-virgin olive oil.

3. Toss potatoes in a light coating of olive oil, oregano, salt, and pepper and cover the bottom level of the baking dish.

4. Toss eggplant in a light coating of olive oil, oregano, salt, and pepper and cover the potatoes to form the next level of the composition.

5. Toss zucchini in a light coating of olive oil, oregano, salt, and pepper and layer on top of the eggplant.

6. Top with red peppers, garlic, and parsley. Add onion quarters. Sprinkle with additional oregano, salt, and pepper.

7. Pour crushed tomatoes to cover the composition and drizzle with Mistra Estates extra-virgin olive oil, 5-6 tbsp (depending on the size of the oven dish).

8. Bake for 45 minutes to 1 hour.

⚘Roasted! Fall and Winter Midwest Vegetables

Duane and Karen Ehrens, RD

Duane is a chef, foodservice director, and cooking instructor. Karen is a Registered Dietitian, connector of dots. Together they teach "Mediterranean on the Prairie" and other cooking classes featuring local foods.

Use the fall root vegetables and squashes that are available to you, in the combinations you like. We find that roasted vegetables can be a "gateway" for those who say they do not care to eat vegetables!

YIELD ~ Varies
PREP TIME ~ 5-20 minutes (depending on choice of vegetables)
TOTAL TIME ~ 45-60 minutes (depending on choice of vegetables)

INGREDIENTS

- Peeled squash, unpeeled potatoes and sweet potatoes, peeled carrots and parsnips, peeled rutabagas, beets, onions, celery root. These all take beautifully to roasting. Use your favorites, or what you have on hand, in any combination. For best results, cut vegetables of the same kind in a uniform size, about 1- inch squares.
- Extra-virgin olive oil
- Salt and pepper
- Spices! (see below)

(A medium butternut squash yields about 3 cups, diced. Three medium carrots or parsnips yield about 1 ½ cups, diced.)

SPICE IT UP!

For 6 cups diced vegetables, try:
- 2 tsp finely chopped rosemary or ½ tsp dried rosemary and roasted garlic -OR-
- 2 tsp curry powder and 3 tsp garam masala for flavors of India -OR-

65

- 1 ½ tsp chili powder and 1 tsp ground cumin for flavors of the Southwest -OR-
- Sprinkle 2 tbsp chopped Italian parsley over vegetables after roasting and before serving.

DIRECTIONS

1. Preheat oven to 400° F. Coat a large baking sheet with cooking spray, or cover sheet with parchment paper.
2. Combine cut vegetables with a small amount of extra-virgin olive oil in a large bowl and toss to coat. Sprinkle salt and pepper and spices onto the vegetables, if you like. Spread the vegetables onto prepared baking sheet(s).
3. Roast in oven until tender when poked with a fork, stirring about every 10 minutes, for a total of about 35 minutes.
4. Remove from oven and enjoy!

ADDITIONAL NOTES

- To add an extra boost of flavor, roast a head of garlic, mash it, and mix it with the other roasted vegetables. (Roast by cutting the tip off the head of garlic, set on a square of foil, sprinkle with a tbsp of water and pinch the edges of the foil together. Place the packet in a 400° F oven, and bake for about 35-45 minutes. When it is done, it will yield to the touch. Unwrap the garlic and let cool slightly. Squeeze the garlic cloves into a small bowl, add 1 tbsp olive oil, and mash with a fork.)
- If you are roasting beets to mix with other veggies, roast on a separate pan or they can share their lovely color with all the others; toss them in to mix just before serving.
- Do not crowd chopped vegetables too closely on the pan when roasting; if you do, you will be steaming the vegetables rather than roasting. We place about 3 cups of diced vegetables per half-sheet pan (18x13 inches).

Ιμ'αμ-Μπαϊαντ'ι – Ιμάμ Βαyιlδί ("Fainting Imam," Stuffed Eggplant)

Giannis Ladopoulos
Connoisseur, Olive Oil Producer, Businessman

This traditional dish of stuffed eggplant is one that our grandmother used to cook during the summer using vegetables from our garden and pure extra-virgin olive oil from our fields.

YIELD ~ 6-8 servings
PREP TIME ~ 1 hour
TOTAL TIME ~ 2 ½ - 3 hours

INGREDIENTS

For the Eggplants:

- 8 eggplants (Tsakoniki is the type that our grandmother grew, but any long eggplant will work.)
- 2 tbsp extra-virgin olive oil
- Salt and black pepper
- 1 tbsp thyme

For the Filling:

- 4 large onions
- 4 tbsp olive oil
- 6 cloves garlic
- 1 tbsp granulated sugar
- ½ tbsp cumin
- Salt and pepper
- 1 tbsp tomato paste
- 8 ounces crushed tomatoes
- 1 tbsp thyme

For Assembly:

- 8-ounce block of feta, sliced
- Black pepper

- Extra-virgin olive oil

For Serving:

- ⅓ bunch parsley, coarsely chopped
- Lettuce (something a little spicy or bitter works well, such as rocket or arugula)
- Black pepper
- Extra-virgin olive oil

DIRECTIONS

1. Preheat the oven to 350° F.

2. Mix the extra-virgin olive oil, salt, pepper, and thyme in a small dish. With a paring knife, make 3 horizontal incisions about halfway deep on one side of each eggplant. Open the incisions a little by sliding your fingers through, being careful not to break the eggplants. Arrange the eggplants in a deep pan, cut side up. In the cuts, put the seasoned olive oil mixture. Bake for 30-40 minutes, depending on the size of your eggplants.

3. Meanwhile, cut the onions into thin slices and finely chop the garlic, keeping it separate from the onions.

4. Put a large skillet on high heat. Once it is very hot, add 4 tbsp extra-virgin olive oil and the onions. When they begin to turn translucent, add the garlic. When the onions start to brown, add the sugar, cumin, salt, pepper, and tomato paste all at once. Sauté on medium heat until the onions are caramelized. Finally, add the crushed tomato and thyme and stir. Simmer for 5 minutes and remove from heat.

5. Remove the eggplants from the oven and run a spoon down each slice to make slots for the filling.

6. Stuff each slot with the onion filling. Place the slices of feta on top, drizzle with the olive oil, and sprinkle with black pepper. Bake for 15-20 minutes until the cheese starts to brown.

7. To serve, spread the lettuce on the serving plate and put the eggplants on top. Sprinkle the chopped parsley, pepper, and olive oil over each eggplant and enjoy.

Patatas Bravas (Spicy Potatoes)

Sam Wai
Traveler, Connoisseur, Wine Educator

Patatas Bravas (Spicy Potatoes), originated in Madrid, is in the tapas category of Spanish cuisine. Today it is ubiquitous in all of Spain. It is pan-fried potato cubes dressed with a spicy, peppery tomato sauce. No two plates of patatas bravas are the same which means you have lots of room to vary to your taste. Many also drizzle a garlicky aioli along with the tomato sauce.

YIELD ~ 4 appetizer portions or as a side dish
PREP TIME ~ 15 minutes
TOTAL TIME ~ 40 minutes

INGREDIENTS

For the Sauce:

- 1 tbsp olive oil
- 1 cup onion, chopped
- 2 cloves garlic, chopped
- ¼ cup white wine
- 1½ cups chopped and skinned tomato
- 2 tsp white or red wine vinegar
- ½ tsp crushed dried chilies (may vary to taste)
- 2 tsp sweet pimentón (may substitute paprika)
- Salt to taste

For the Potatoes:

- 4 large potatoes, washed and cut into ¾ inch cubes (peeling them is optional)
- 3 tbsp olive oil
- Salt and pepper to taste

DIRECTIONS

1. Sauté chopped onions in 1 tbsp of olive oil gently for 5 minutes, but not to brown.

2. Add the garlic and cook for two minutes, but not to brown.

3. Add the rest of the ingredients for the sauce, let it come to a boil and reduce heat to a simmer for 10-15 minutes until it is reduced to a sauce the consistency of gravy.

4. Use a hand-held blender, a regular blender, or a food processor to blend until smooth.

5. Pan fry the cubed potatoes in olive oil until the pieces are a light golden brown and cooked through, about 20 minutes. Adjust the amount of oil as needed.

6. Season potatoes with salt and pepper to taste.

7. Drizzle on the spicy tomato sauce and serve at once.

VARIATIONS

You may also add a spicy aioli by adding garlic powder, lemon juice, and a pinch of cayenne pepper to half a cup of mayonnaise. Drizzle on the potatoes along with the tomato sauce.

DAIRY-FREE ITALIAN STUFFED BELL PEPPERS

Kayla Coté van Rensburg
Designer, Podcaster, Health Enthusiast

Kayla Coté van Rensburg is a health and wellness enthusiast in the Fargo community. Her mission is to help people live well, be well, and discover their WoW factor. She is delighted to share recipes that are as healthy as they are delicious. Kayla believes food can be simple and fun and has the power to help shape a happy, healthy life. To eat well is to be well. Give yourself the gift of enjoying good food.

YIELD ~ 4 servings
PREP TIME ~ 20 minutes
TOTAL TIME ~ 50 minutes

INGREDIENTS

- 2 large red bell peppers
- Extra-virgin olive oil
- ¼ raw sweet potato, diced
- ½ medium red onion, diced
- ½ cup chickpeas, rinsed and drained
- 1 celery rib, diced
- ½ cup red cabbage, roughly chopped
- ½ cup cooked quinoa
- 2 cloves garlic, minced
- ½ cup grape tomatoes, halved
- 1-2 tbsp blend of Italian herbs
- 2 tbsp balsamic vinegar
- Sea salt and cracked pepper, to taste
- 1 bunch fresh basil, roughly chopped
- Juice of ½ lemon
- ½ avocado, thinly sliced

DIRECTIONS

1. Preheat the oven to 425° F. Cut red bell pepper in half and remove seeds and stem. Brush the cut edge and inside with olive oil. Put the peppers cut side facing up on the pan, season with sea salt.

2. In separate pan, add 1 tbsp extra-virgin olive oil, sweet potato, onion, chickpeas, celery, red cabbage, tomatoes, garlic, herbs, and balsamic vinegar. Add salt and cracked pepper to taste.

3. Put both pans in the oven and cook for 20-30 minutes or until veggies are cooked and balsamic has slightly caramelized onto the veggies.

4. Pull the roasted vegetables pan out of the oven. Turn oven to broil for 5-8 minutes, checking frequently, until peppers are charred to your liking. Remove from oven.

5. In a large bowl, add roasted vegetables to the quinoa, lemon juice, and chopped basil. Mix well.

6. Plate roasted red peppers and stuff with veggie-quinoa mixture. Top with cracked pepper and serve warm or cold. Garnish with 2 to 3 avocado slices.

7. This recipe can be eaten as a meal, or can be paired with a roasted salmon fillet and a white wine such as Pinot Grigio or Sauvignon Blanc.

❧ Corfu Rooster with Bucatini Pasta

Gary Litt

Scholar, Traveler, Gentleman

Corfu is an island off Greece's northwest coast in the Ionian Sea. Corfu rooster or chicken is a delicious dish enjoyed frequently as a Sunday meal to share with family and friends. If you can get a rooster, it will require a long cooking time, 2+ hours, but it's worth the wait for the exceptional flavor. Regular chicken will work; just cook for an hour or so.

YIELD ~ 6-8 servings
PREP TIME ~ 1 hour
TOTAL TIME ~ 2 ½ - 3 hours

INGREDIENTS

- 1 whole, large chicken (cockerel/rooster), cut into pieces. You can also use chicken thighs, bone in and skin on or a whole, regularly sized chicken (approx. 3-3½ lbs). Beef also works.
- 4-6 tbsp of olive oil
- 2 onions, chopped
- 4 cloves of garlic, minced
- Salt and pepper to taste
- 1 tsp cinnamon
- ½ tsp ground clove
- 1 tsp paprika
- 1 tsp grated nutmeg
- 1 tsp ground cumin
- 6 all-spice berries
- 1 tsp lemon pepper seasoning
- 2 tsp granulated roasted garlic (This is a bit hard to find; I buy it at Penzeys or other good spice stores.)
- ½ tsp ground Chipotle pepper

- 1+ tsp turkey soup base (I prefer Penzeys, but a good chicken/turkey stock/paste will do.)
- ½ of 1, 14.5-ounce can fire-roasted, diced tomatoes
- 2 tbsp tomato paste
- 2+ tsp good balsamic vinegar (depending on the acidity of the tomatoes)
- ½ cup red wine
- 1 cup chicken broth
- 2 bay leaves
- 1, 12-ounce package bucatini pasta (or another type of pasta or potatoes, mashed or boiled)
- Grated cheese of choice, for serving
- Chopped fresh herbs for garnish — parsley or basil work well

DIRECTIONS

1. Preheat oven to 350° F .
2. Dry chicken pieces with paper towel and season with salt, pepper, and granulated roasted garlic.
3. In a heavy-bottom stewing pot or Dutch oven, heat oil to medium-high and brown chicken in batches skin side down first and then all sides. Remove and set aside.
4. Reduce heat to medium, add the onions, and sauté until tender and translucent, about 5 minutes. Add the garlic and all the spices except the bay leaf. Cook until fragrant.
5. Stir in the tomato paste and cook for 30 seconds. Add the wine and let it cook and reduce for a minute.
6. Add the tomatoes, broth, and bay leaf. Give everything a stir, then carefully place the chicken in the pot with the sauce (coming about halfway up the chicken or more).
7. Bring the sauce to a boil. Once at a boil, place in the oven and cook for 1 ½ to 2 hours or more, depending on your chicken, stirring occasionally. The time depends upon the chicken. If you have a rooster, it will take up to 2 hours or more; if it is an

ordinary chicken, or thighs, it will cook in an hour or so. Use a meat thermometer to register that the rooster/chicken has reached 165° F.

8. Remove from oven and adjust for seasoning.

9. Return Dutch oven to the stovetop and turn heat to medium.

10. Stir in balsamic vinegar to taste and allow sauce to simmer and reduce until it is nice and thick, another 10 minutes if needed.

11. In the meantime, cook your pasta according to package directions in salted boiling water. Drain and add butter or drizzle of olive oil.

12. To serve: Plate pasta on individual plates or a serving platter topped with the chicken and sauce. Sprinkle with freshly grated cheese and some chopped fresh herbs.

MEDITERRANEAN SPAGHETTI WITH LOBSTER

David Clardy, MD
Sanford Health

This is one of my all-time favorites and reminds me of my time in the Greek islands with my good friends. I can make this in less than half an hour and it serves four people. It really needs to be paired with a crisp white wine, ideally an assyrtiko from Santorini.

YIELD ~ 6-8 servings
PREP TIME ~ 30 minutes
COOK TIME ~ 30 minutes

INGREDIENTS

- 12 ounces spaghetti
- Kosher salt
- 2 tbsp cold-pressed, extra-virgin olive oil
- 1 large shallot, finely chopped
- 2 cloves garlic, minced
- 2 tsp tomato paste
- 1 tsp crushed red pepper flakes
- ½ tsp paprika
- ⅓ cup sweet vermouth
- 2 tbsp unsalted butter
- 1 pound picked cooked lobster meat (or large shrimp)
- Freshly ground black pepper
- 1 tsp grated lemon zest
- 2 tsp fresh parsley
- Lemon wedges, for serving

1. In a large pot of boiling salted water, cook spaghetti per package directions until almost al dente. Drain pasta, reserving 1 cup of the cooking liquid.

2. Heat olive oil in a large skillet over medium-high heat. Cook shallot and garlic until softened, about 2 minutes. Add tomato paste, red pepper flakes, and paprika, cook for 1 minute. Add vermouth and cook until reduced by half, about 2 minutes. Simmer another 2-3 minutes, then add butter.

3. Add lobster meat to skillet and toss to coat. Add pasta and ¼ cup reserved pasta water. Toss together constantly and add more pasta water as needed until the sauce thickens. Season with salt and pepper.

4. Top with lemon zest and parsley with lemon wedges on the side of each serving.

🌿 GASTRIN, A TRADITIONAL MINOAN DESSERT

Georgios Maltezakis
Owner, Tasting Crete

Crete is an island with incredible culinary depth. It's also the cradle of European civilization and the home of ancient Minoan culture, one of the first societies to scale the production of olive oil, barley, and wine – and to trade it with neighboring regions. Crete is also a modern culinary mecca due in part to the prevalence of tourism. Crete thus rests at the crossroads of both time and geography – between the millennia, between three continents, and between two oceans.

Despite the varying influences, Cretans have managed to preserve a culinary identity that is both distinct and nutritionally complete. Desserts of the island highlight the characteristic traits of Cretan food habits; they're based on simple ingredients and are entirely unique. Gastrin seems to have truly ancient, Minoan origins. (For many, gastrin is considered the father of baklava; we first find a mention of gastrin as a dessert in Athenaeus's Deipnosophistae in the 3rd century A.D.) What better to include in a volume exploring modern possibilities of an ancient diet. This recipe is translated and recorded as passed on to me by my mother, Georgia. A gastrin dessert is best finished with a shot of Cretan raki or sweet liatiko!

YIELD ~ 12+ servings
PREP TIME ~ 1 hour
TOTAL TIME ~ 2 hours

INGREDIENTS

For the Dough:

- 500 grams (4 cups) all-purpose flour
- 1 tsp salt
- 50 ml cold-pressed, extra-virgin olive oil (about 3 tbsp + 1 tsp)
- Juice from 1 lemon
- 250 ml water (about 1 cup)
- 100 grams sesame seeds, ground

You can always buy pre-made phyllo pastry from the market and use it instead.

For the Filling:

- 300 grams hazelnuts, ground
- 300 grams almonds, roasted and ground
- 4 tbsp olive oil
- 300 grams walnuts, ground
- 100 grams sesame seeds, roasted
- 100 grams poppy seeds
- ½ tsp sweet pepper (ground black pepper)
- ½ cup honey

  Nuts should be ground, but not into powder. We need texture from the nuts.

For the Syrup:

- 2 cups sugar
- 1 cup water
- 1 cup petimezi (grape syrup) *alternatively, you can use maple syrup or, even better, carob syrup*
- 1 cup honey
- 2 tbsp lemon juice

DIRECTIONS

1. Preheat oven to 350° F.
2. For the dough, add the flour to a bowl and make a hole in the middle so it is easier to make the mixture. Add the rest of the ingredients and start mixing. Once you create a soft and non-sticky dough, divide it into three equal parts.
3. Roll the dough into three equally sized sheets. You want the dough as thin as possible so it will offer a crunchy yet soft sensation. (Alternatively, you can always go with a phyllo pastry pack from your local store.)
4. For the filling, pour all ingredients into a bowl and mix well.

5. Cover the bottom of a 25x35 cm (9x13") pan with a little olive oil and lay one of the pastry sheets on the bottom.

6. Spread half of the filling on top of the dough.

7. Add the next sheet of dough, brush with olive oil, and top with the rest of the filling.

8. Cover with the remaining dough and brush again with olive oil.

9. Sprinkle with a little water, carve the cake into rectangular pieces, and in the center of each piece, place a halved walnut.

10. Place in the oven and bake for 40-45 minutes, until light brown and crispy.

11. While the pastry is baking, make the syrup. Put the sugar, water, and syrup in a saucepan and bring to a boil over medium heat for 8 minutes.

12. Add the honey and lemon and mix well until the honey dissolves in the syrup. Let cool.

13. Once cool, pour the syrup over the baked pastry and let it absorb completely.

14. Cut pieces as marked, serve, and enjoy!

Note: The Mediterranean diet recommends sugar and processed grains to be limited. It is best to enjoy desserts like this on special occasions and in small portions. It also can be accompanied by fresh fruit like apples, pears, mandarins, or stone fruits.

Blackboard Olive Oil Lemon Bundt Cake with Lemon Curd and Lavender Cream Cheese Icing

Terri Trickle
Blackboard

YIELD ~ (5) Mini fluted cakes *OR* (1) 8″ fluted tube cake *OR* (1) 8 ½″ x 4 ½″ loaf
PREP TIME ~ 10 minutes
COOKING TIME ~ 24 minutes

INGREDIENTS

For the Cake:

- 3 large eggs
- 4 tbsp heavy cream or milk
- 2 tsp vanilla
- 1 ½ cups sifted flour
- ½ cup sugar
- Grated zest of one lemon
- ½ tsp baking powder
- ¼ tsp salt
- 8 tbsp butter (one stick)
- 3 tbsp olive oil
- Poppy seeds
- Sea salt flakes

For the Lemon Syrup:

- ½ cup sugar
- Juice of two whole lemons (strained)

For the Lemon Curd:

- 3 large eggs
- ½ cup sugar

- Grated zest of one lemon
- 1.2 cups strained fresh lemon juice (about 2 lemons)
- 6 tbsp butter, cut into small pieces

For the Lavender Cream Cheese Frosting:
- 8 ounces cream cheese (one block)
- 5 tbsp unsalted butter, softened
- 2 tsp lavender extract (available at baking stores and online)
- 1 pound (4 cups) confectioners' sugar

DIRECTIONS

1. Have all ingredients at room temperature, heat the oven to 350° F. Grease and flour pan. Line a loaf pan bottom with wax paper. For a mini-fluted pan, spray with cooking spray.

2. In a medium bowl, whisk together eggs, heavy cream, and vanilla.

3. In a large bowl, whisk together flour, sugar, lemon zest, baking powder, and salt.

4. Add half of the egg mixture to the flour mixture, along with butter and Mistra Estates extra-virgin olive oil.

5. Beat on low speed until the dry ingredients are moistened. Increase the speed to high and beat for one minute. Gradually add the rest of the egg mixture and scrape the sides of the bowl. Scrape batter into prepared pan(s), spreading evenly. Sprinkle with poppy seeds and sea salt flakes.

6. Bake in the center of the oven until a toothpick inserted into the center comes out clean. 24 minutes for mini pans, 35 to 45 minutes in a fluted-tube pan, 55 minutes for a loaf.

7. Meanwhile, shortly before cake(s) are done, combine ½ cup sugar and juice of two lemons in a small saucepan and stir over low heat until the sugar is dissolved.

8. As soon as the cake comes out of the oven, place the pan on a rack, poke the cake all over with a wooden skewer (a couple of

toothpicks are fine too), and brush it with half the syrup. Let cool in the pan on a wire rack for 10 minutes.

9. Slide a slim knife around the sides of the fluted-tube pan against the counter to loosen the cake. Invert onto a greased rack and peel off the paper liner. Poke the bottom and sides of the cake with the skewer and brush with the remainder of the syrup. Let cool completely, right side up or inverted when wrapped airtight, and chill for 24 hours before serving.

10. To make the curd: Whisk together eggs, sugar, lemon zest, fresh lemon juice, and butter in a medium stainless steel or enamel saucepan until light in color. Cook, whisking, over medium heat until the butter is melted. Then whisk constantly until the mixture is thickened and simmers gently for a few seconds. Using the spatula, scrape the filling into a medium mesh sieve set over a bowl and strain the filling into the bowl. Let cool, cover, and refrigerate to thicken. (At Blackboard, we make these as mini fluted cakes and fill the center with our fresh lemon curd.)

11. To make the lavender cream cheese frosting: Beat cream cheese, butter, and lavender extract in a medium bowl at low speed until just blended. Add confectioners' sugar one third at a time and beat just until smooth and the desired consistency. If the frosting is too stiff, beat for a few seconds longer. Place frosting in piping bag with fluted tip and ice around the top of the cakes.

Note: The Mediterranean diet recommends sugar and processed grains to be limited. It is best to enjoy desserts like this on special occasions and in small portions. It also can be accompanied by fresh fruit.

 # Appendix B

How Do You Buy the Very Best Extra-Virgin Olive Oil?

Peter Schultz, PhD

In 2011, Tom Mueller published his book *Extra Virginity. The Sublime and Scandalous World of Olive Oil.* This book followed closely on the heels of a (now infamous!) 2010 report on "extra-virgin olive oil" by scholars from the Davis Olive Oil Center at the Robert Mondavi Institute for Wine and Food Science and the University of California, Davis. The conclusion of these important publications was identical: The world of olive oil is rife with inaccuracies, half-truths, and fraud.

The UC, Davis study concludes:

> Of the five top-selling imported "extra-virgin" olive oil brands in the United States, 73 percent of the samples *failed* the IOC sensory standards for extra-virgin olive oils analyzed by two IOC-accredited sensory panels. The failure rate ranged from a high of 94 percent to a low of 56 percent depending on the brand and the panel. None of the Australian and California samples failed both sensory panels, while 11 percent of the top-selling premium Italian brand samples failed the two panels. Sensory defects are indicators that these samples are oxidized, of poor quality, and/or adulterated with cheaper refined oils.

In the last decade or so, this research has been substantiated time and time again, leaving all of us who love the Mediterranean diet with a serious question: *How do you buy the very best extra-virgin olive oil?*

The good news is that this is a very easy question to answer!

Here's a fast, fun, fact-based checklist of three key criteria that you can use to find and buy the highest quality extra-virgin olive oil.

1. Your extra-virgin olive oil should always come in ceramic, in dark glass, or in a stainless-steel tin; it should never be stored a clear bottle — and it should never come in plastic.

Photons — light — degrade the quality of extra-virgin olive oil. Indeed, any exposure to light can cause a substantial loss of key antioxidants, especially tocopherols, and an increase in rancidity compared to oil stored in the dark. For this reason, an opaque or dark container is a must.

A glass or steel container is also very important. In 2018, Maryam Hooshyari and her colleagues at the Università degli Studi di Genova conducted a series of studies which showed that olive oil stored in plastic bottles or bags undergoes far more rapid oxidation due to the permeability of PET (polyethylene terephthalate) plastic. Plastics also contains BPA (bisphenol A). BPA is an industrial chemical that has been used to make popular plastics and resins since the 1960s. Polycarbonate plastics are often used in containers that store food and beverages, such as water bottles. They may also be used in other consumer goods. Epoxy resins are used to coat the inside of metal products, such as food cans, bottle tops, and water supply lines. Research has shown that BPA can seep into food or beverages from containers that are made with BPA. Exposure to BPA is a concern because of possible health effects of BPA on the brain and prostate glands of fetuses, infants, and children. It can also affect children's behavior. Additional research suggests a possible link between BPA and increased blood pressure. Ceramic, glass, or steel are the best ways to go.

2. Your extra-virgin olive oil's label should always display a harvest and/or season date and a documented acidity level.

Research has shown that it takes next to nothing for an unscrupulous manufacturer to label an oil "cold-pressed" or "extra-virgin." Also, even olive oil that is technically "extra-virgin" can spoil, especially when it's brought into the United States in multi-ton bulk orders and stored for long periods of time in shipping containers, warehouses, or grocery stores. Acidity level is also a key indicator of quality and should always be shown on the label.

The two best ways to address this concern is to be sure that (1) the label of your extra-virgin olive oil is marked with a harvest date and, (2) that the label of your extra-virgin olive oil is marked with a documented level of acidity.

With regards to date, it's important to remember that olive oil is a seasonal product. In the northern hemisphere, the olive harvest usually takes between October and January. Here in the U.S., the very freshest olive oil from a harvest year will arrive in the late spring and summer. While it can last 3-4 years when stored in a cool, dry place, an olive oil's very best flavor will manifest within two years of the harvest date. (Truly fresh extra-virgin olive oil is almost a miracle to taste; once you have, it's almost impossible to go back.) Be sure that when you're looking at your oil's harvest date that it's not more than two years old.

With regards to acidity, less is always more. The lower acidity, the better. In order to technically qualify as "extra-virgin olive oil," an oil must have an acidity of less than 0.8%. Anything below this number is a good product. Extra-virgin olive oils with a range of 0-0.6% acidity are some of the very best in the world. Tasting an early pressing of green olives at 0.0% acidity can be life-changing.

3. Your extra-virgin olive oil should always come from a single farm or a regional co-op. In other words, know who grows and harvests your food.

The vast majority of extra-virgin olive oil in the supermarket is comprised of industrial blends derived from multiple production sites and even multiple countries. The goals of these producers are volume and economies of scale. These goals are entirely fine, of course, but they're incompatible with elite quality. If you want the very best extra-virgin olive oil in the world, then buy from a family farm or a regional co-op. These outfits usually take great care of their land, guarantee the freshest products in the world, and take enormous pride in the quality of their oil. Even more important, discovering high quality farms is a blast and building relationships with the people who grow and make what you eat will always have rewards that go far beyond mere sustenance. It's quite easy to find high quality olive oil of this sort. The internet offers a vast range of local growers and, if you're up in the High Plains of the American Midwest, you can always sign up for our annual order of Mistra Estates Extra-Virgin Olive Oil at www.peterschultzimporter.com!

# SELECT BIBLIOGRAPHY

CHAPTER ONE
A BRIEF PREHISTORY OF THE MEDITERRANEAN DIET

Altomare, Roberta, Francesco Cacciabaudo, Giuseppe Damiano, Vincenzo Davide Palumbo, Maria Concetta Giovale, Maurizio Bellavia, Giovanni Tomasello, and Attilio Ignazio Lo Monte. "The Mediterranean Diet: A History of Health." *Iran J Public Health* 42, no. 5.: 449-57.

Fallon Morell, Sally. *Nourishing Diets: How Paleo, Ancestral, and Traditional Ancestors Really Ate.* New York: Grand Central Life & Style, 2018.

Koh, A.J., and P.P. Betancourt. Wine and Olive Oil from an Early Minoan I Hilltop Fort. *Mediterranean Archaeology and Archaeometry* 10, no. 2: 15-23.

Mercader, Julio. "Mozambican Grass Seed Consumption During the Middle Stone Age." *Science* 326, no. 5960: 1680-83.

Namdar, Dvory, Alon Amrani, Nimrod Getzov, and Ianir Milevski. "Olive Oil Storage During the Fifth and Sixth Millenia BC at Ein Zippori, Northern Israel." *Israel Journal of Plant Sciences* 62, 1-2 (2015): 65-74.

Nesbitt, Mark, and Delwen Samuel. "From Staple Crop to Extinction? The Archaeology and History of the Hulled Wheats." In *Hulled Wheats: Proceedings of the First International Workshop on Hulled Wheats*, edited by S. Padulosi, K. Hammer, and J. Heller, 41-100. Rome: IPGRI, 1995.

O'Connor, Sue, Mahirta, Sofía C. Samper Carro, Stuart Hawkins, Shimona Kealy, Julien Louys, and Rachel Wood. "Fishing in Life and Death: Pleistocene Fish-hooks from Burial Context on Alor Island, Indonesia." *Antiquity* 91, no. 360: 1451-68.

Preedy, Victor R., and Ronald Ross Watson, eds. *The Mediterranean Diet: An Evidence-Based Approach.* Amsterdam: Academic Press, 2014.

Riccomi, Giulia. *Bioarchaeology and Dietary Reconstruction Across Late Antiquity and the Middle Ages in Tuscany, Central Italy.* Oxford: Archaeopress Archaeology, 2021.

Stiner, Mary C. "The Faunas of Hayonim Cave, Israel: A 200,000-Year Record of Paleolithic Diet, Demography, and Society." *Journal of Anthropological Research* 63, no. 2: 275-77.

Tanasi, Davide, Enrico Greco, Radwan Ebna Noor, Stephanie Feola, Vasantha Kumar, Anita Crispino, and Ioannis Gelis. "1H NMR, 1H-1H 2D TOCSY and GC-MS Analyses for the Identification of Olive Oil on Early Bronze Age Pottery from Castelluccio (Noto, Italy)." *Analytical Methods* no. 10, 2757: 1-8.

Zilhão, J., et. al. "Last Interglacial Iberian Neandertals as Fisher-Hunter-Gatherers." *Science* 367, no. 6485. DOI: 10.1126/science.aaz7943.

CHAPTER TWO
HEALTHY EATING WITH FOODS & FLAVORS OF THE MEDITERRANEAN

Bloom, Jonathan. *American Wasteland: How America Throws Away Nearly Half of Its Food (And What We Can Do About It.)* Boston: Da Capo Lifelong Books, 2011.

Gunders, D. *Wasted: How America is Losing Up to 40% of Its Food from Farm to Fork to Landfill.* Washington, D.C.: Natural Resources Defense Council, 2012.

McManus, Katherine. "A Practical Guide to the Mediterranean Diet." *Harvard Health Blog* (blog). *Harvard Health Publishing*, March 21, 2019. https://www.health.harvard.edu/blog/a-practical-guide-to-the-mediterranean-diet-2019032116194.

Oldways Cultural Food Traditions. "Mediterranean Diet." Accessed March 2021. https://www.oldwayspt.org/traditional-diets/mediterranean-diet.

The Bean Institute. "Nutrition & Health Benefits." https://www.beaninstitute.com.

U.S. Department of Health & Human Services and U.S. Department of Agriculture. *2020 – 2025 Dietary Guidelines for Americans.* 9th Edition. December 2020. https://www.dietaryguidelines.gov.

CHAPTER THREE
FARMING FOR FLAVOR IN THE UPPER MIDWEST

Khalaf, Eyada Mohammed. "Phenolic-Linked Antioxidant and Anti-Hyperglycemic Properties of Selected Cereal, Pseudo-Cereal, and Millet Using In Vitro Screening Methods." Master's thesis, North Dakota State University, 2018.

Mishra, L.K., D. Sarkar, S. Zwinger, and K. Shetty. "Phenolic Anitoxidant-Linked Hyperglycemic Properties of Rye Cultivars Grown Under Conventional and Organic Production Systems." *Journal of Cereal Science* 76: 108-15.

Zwinger, Steve, Steve Schaubert, and Jim Eckberg. "Intercropping Oats and Field Pea in an Organic Production System." *CREC Annual Report* 60: 17-20.

CHAPTER FOUR
YOUR MENTAL HEALTH AND THE MEDITERRANEAN DIET

Auquier, Pascal, Stéphane Robitail, Pierre-Michel Llorca, and Benoît Rive. "Comparison of Escitalopram and Citalopram Efficacy: A Meta-Analysis." *International Journal of Psychiatry in Clinical Practice* 7, no. 4: 259-68.

Braun, C., A. Adams, L. Rink, T. Bschor, K. Kuhr, and C. Baethge. "In Search of a Dose–Response Relationship in SSRIs — A Systematic Review, Meta-Analysis, and Network Meta-Analysis." *Acta Psychiatrica Scandinavica* 142, no. 6: 430-42.

Gaab, Jens, Cosima Locher, and Charlotte Blease. "Placebo and Psychotherapy: Differences, Similarities, and Implications." *International Review of Neurobiology* 138: 241-55.

Helgadóttir, Björg, Mats Hallgren, Örjan Ekblom, and Yvonne Forsell. "Training Fast or Slow? Exercise for Depression: A Randomized Controlled Trial." *Preventive Medicine* 91: 123-31.

Jacka, Felice N., Adrienne O'Neil, Rachelle Opie, Catherine Itsiopoulos, Sue Cotton, Mohammedreza Mohebbi, David Castle, et al. "A Randomised Controlled Trial of Dietary Improvement for Adults with Major Depression (The 'SMILES' Trial)."*BMC Medicine* 15, no. 1: 1-13.

Kris-Etherton, Penny M, Kristina S. Petersen, Joseph R. Hibbeln, Daniel Hurley, Valerie Kolick, Sevetra Peoples, Nancy Rodriguez, and Gail Woodward-Lopez. "Nutrition and Behavioral Health Disorders: Depression and Anxiety." *Nutrition Reviews* 79, no. 3: 247-60.

Luty, Suzanne E., Janet D. Carter, Janice M. McKenzie, Alma M. Rae, Christopher M.A. Frampton, Roger T. Mulder, and Peter R. Joyce. "Randomised Controlled Trial of Interpersonal Psychotherapy and Cognitive–Behavioural Therapy for Depression." *The British Journal of Psychiatry* 190, no. 6: 496-502.

Martins, Lais B., Jenneffer Rayan Braga Tibães, Marsal Sanches, Felice Jacka, Michael Berk, and Antônio L. Teixeira. "Nutrition-Based Interventions for Mood Disorders." *Expert Review of Neurotherapeutics* 21, no. 3: 303-315.

Parletta, Natalie, Dorota Zarnowiecki, Jihyun Cho, Amy Wilson, Svetlana Bogomolova, Anthony Villani, Catherine Itsiopoulos, et al. "A Mediterranean-style Dietary Intervention Supplemented with Fish Oil Improves Diet Quality and Mental Health in People with Depression: A Randomised Controlled Trial (HELFIMED)." *Journal of the Australasian College of Nutritional and Environmental Medicine* 37, no. 1: 6-18.

Svanborg, P., and M. Åsberg. "A Comparison Between the Beck Depression Inventory (BDI) and the Self-Rating Version of the Montgomery Åsberg Depression Rating Scale (MADRS)." *Journal of Affective Disorders* 64, no. 2-3: 203-216.

CHAPTER FIVE
THE MEDITERRANEAN DIET IS GOOD FOR YOUR HEART

Barzi, F., M. M. Woodward, R.M. Marfisi, L. Tavazzi, F. Valagussa, and R. Marchioli. "Mediterranean Diet and All-causes Mortality After Myocardial Infarction: Results from the GISSI-Prevenzione Trial." *European Journal of Clinical Nutrition* 57: 604-11.

Bonaccio, Marialaura, et. al. "Mediterranean Diet and Mortality in the Elderly: A Prospective Cohort Study and a Meta-analysis." *British Journal of Nutrition* (2018): 1-14.

Buettner, Dan. *The Blue Zones, 9 Lessons for Living Longer.* 2nd ed. Washington D.C.: National Geographic Society, 2012.

——. *Blue Zones Solution, Eating and Living Like the World's Healthiest People.* Reprint, Washington, D.C.: National Geographic Society, 2017.

Casas, R., E. Sacanella, and R. Estruch. "The Immune Protective Effect of the Mediterranean Diet against Chronic Low-grade Inflammatory Diseases." *Endocrine, Metabolic and Immune Disorders - Drug Targets* 14, no. 4: 245-54.

De Lorgeril, M., P. Salen, J.L. Martin, I. Monjaud, J. Delaye, and N. Mamelle. "Mediterranean Diet, Traditional Risk Factors, and the Rate of Cardiovascular Complications after Myocardial Infarction: Final Report of the Lyon Diet Heart Study." *Circulation* 99: 779-85.

Esposito, Katherine, et. al. "The Mediterranean Diet and the Metabolic Syndrome." *Journal of the American Medical Association* 292: 1440-46.

Estruch, Ramón, et. al. "Primary Prevention of Cardiovascular Disease with a Mediterranean Diet Supplemented with Extra-Virgin Olive Oil or Nuts." *New England Journal of Medicine* 378, no. 34 (2018).

Fuhrman, Joel. *Eat To Live: The Amazing Nutrient-Rich Program for Fast and Sustained Weight Loss.* Revised ed., London: Confer Books, 2011.

Knoops, Kim T.B., et. al. "Mediterranean Diet, Lifestyle Factors, and 10-Year Mortality in Elderly European Men and Women: The HALE Project." *Journal of the American Medical Association* 292: 1433-39.

Mitrou, Panagiota N., et. al. "Mediterranean Dietary Pattern and Prediction of All-cause Mortality in a U.S. Population." *Archives of Internal Medicine* 167: 2461-68.

O'Keefe, James H., Neil M. Gheewala, and Joan O. O'Keefe. "Dietary Strategies for Improving Postprandial Glucose, Lipids, Inflammation, and Cardiovascular Health." *Journal of the American College of Cardiology* 51, no. 3: 249-55.

Ozner, Michael. *Heart Attacks Are Not Worth Dying For.* Grove City: Gatekeeper Press, 2021.

——. *The Complete Mediterranean Diet: Everything You Need to Know to Lose Weight and Lower Your Risk of Heart Disease.* Dallas: BenBella Books, 2014.

Samieri, Cécilia, Qi Sun, Mary K. Townsend, Stephanie E. Chiuve, Olivia I. Okereke, Walter C. Willett, Meir Stampfer, and Francine Grodstein. "The Association Between Dietary Patterns at Midlife and Health in Aging: An Observational Study. *Annals of Internal Medicine* 159, no. 9: 584-91.

Willet, W.C., F. Sacks, A. Trichopoulou, G. Drescher, A. Ferro-Luzzi, E. Helsing, D. Trichopoulos. "Mediterranean Diet Pyramid: A Cultural Model for Healthy Eating. *American Journal of Clinical Nutrition* 61, suppl. 6: 1402S-1406S.

Chapter Six
Your Gut and the Mediterranean Diet

Colleen, Alanna. *10% Human: How Your Body's Microbes Hold the Key to Health and Happiness*. New York: Harper, 2016.

Del Chierico, Federica, Pamela Vernocchi, Bruno Dallapiccola, and Lorenza Putignani. "Mediterranean Diet and Health: Food Effects on Gut Microbiota and Disease Control." *International Journal of Molecular Sciences* 15, no. 7: 11678-99.

Finlay, B. Brett, and Jessica Finlay. *The Whole-Body Microbiome; How to Harness Microbes – Inside and Out – for Livelong Health*. New York: The Experiment, 2019.

Gavahian, Mohsen, Amin Mousavi Khaneghah, Jose M. Lorenzon, and Paulo Eduardo Munekata. "Health Benefits of Olive Oil and its Components: Impact on Gut Microbiota, and Prevention of the Risk of Development of Noncommunicable Diseases." *Trends in Food Science & Technology* 88: 220-27.

Knight, Rob. *Follow your Gut: The Enormous Impact of Tiny Microbes*. New York: TED Books, Simon and Schuster: 2015.

Martínez, Nieves, Isabel Prieto, Marina Hidalgo, Ana Belén Segarra, Ana M. Martínez-Rodríguez, Antonio Cobo, Manuel Ramírez, Antonio Gálvez, and Magdalena Martínez-Cañamero. "Refined versus Extra Virgin Olive Oil High-Fat Diet Impact on Intestinal Microbiota of Mice and Its Relation to Different Physiological Variables." *Microorganisms* 7(2), 61. no. 7.

Mayer, Emeran. *The Mind-Gut Connection: How the Hidden Coversation Within Our Bodies Impacts Our Mood, Our Choices, and Our Overall Health.* New York: Harper, 2018.

Prieto, Isabel, Marina Hidalgo, Ana Belén Segarra, and Ana María Martínez-Rodríguez. "Influence of a Diet Enriched with Virgin Olive Oil or Butter on Mouse Gut Microbiota and its Correlation to Physiological and Biochemical Parameters Related to Metabolic Syndrome." *PLoS ONE* 13, no.1.

Tuck, Kellie L., and Peter J. Hayball. "Major Phenolic Compounds in Olive Oil: Metabolism and Health Effect." *The Journal of Nutritional Biochemistry* 13, no. 11: 636-44.

Yong, Ed. *I Contain Multitudes: The Microbes Within Us and a Grander View of Life.* NewYork: Ecco, 2016.

APPENDIX B
HOW DO YOU BUY THE VERY BEST EXTRA VIRGIN OLIVE OIL?

Hooshyari, Maryam, Eleonora Mustorgi, Cristina Malegori, and Paolo Oliveri. "Effect of Storage in Plastic Bottles on the Quality of Extra Virgin Olive Oil." Poster presented at the Giornate Italo-Francesi di Chimica Conference, Genova, Italy, April 16-18, 2018. DOI: 10.13140/RG.2.2.21362.76487.

Mueller, Tom. *Extra Virginity. The Sublime and Scandalous World of Olive Oil.* New York: W.W. Norton & Company, 2013.